The Secret
Of Being Strong

By

C. W. Naylor

AUTHOR OF

"The Secret of the Singing Heart"

THE WARNER PRESS

Anderson   Indiana

PREFACE

IDEAS are powerful and often have a profound effect. But ideas and thoughts that at one time strongly move us have a way of growing dim and losing their force as the seasons succeed each other. This is why they need to be put into print. Books do not forget.

Hundreds of people have told me personally, or have written, that my writings have brought them comfort, strength, and courage. This, and the favorable reception given a volume of similar short miscellaneous topics entitled *Heart Talks*, has moved me to present in permanent form this similar volume with the hope that these messages may have a ministry of blessing to many readers.

These messages have been made quite personal in order that reader and author may draw close together and share together the thoughts and experiences expressed, for life for us all is pretty much alike in its problems, its difficulties, its hopes, and its fears. If in this volume the reader finds something to stimulate, to uplift, and to encourage, the author's hope will have been fulfilled.

C. W. NAYLOR

Anderson, Indiana
August, 1941

CONTENTS

Contents

THE SECRET OF BEING STRONG

SAMSON was a mighty man. He did exploits that no other had done. People were in terror because of him. His enemies sought by every possible means to learn the secret of his great strength. They desired to know it for an evil purpose, that they might subdue him. There are those today who possess spiritual strength that sometimes amazes people as much as the strength of Samson amazed the people of his time. People sometimes inquire the secret of this strength that they themselves may acquire strength. Some are strong to endure. Some are strong to accomplish. Some are mighty to resist evil. We read of those who "out of weakness are made strong." Perhaps we have seen examples of those who had been weak but who suddenly became towers of strength. Or, perhaps their increase of strength came gradually. We look upon them and desire to be like them. We may be like them. We are commanded to be strong, and no impossibility is laid upon us. We may

7

be strong, but in order to be strong, we must learn the secret of strength.

The first thing in being strong is to come to a realization of our own strength. There is within each one of us an unconquerable will. Will power is one of the mightiest of all forces. You may feel weak. You may feel that you have few, if any, of the elements that will enable you to conquer. Your will may seem to be weak, but it is not weak. If it does not accomplish the desired result, it is because you do not use its strength—not because it has no strength. The human will cannot be coerced. Our fellow men cannot compel us. They can force no compliance of our will to their desires. If our will yields, it yields of its own choice. Satan cannot coerce our wills any more than we can coerce his. God himself cannot coerce our wills. If our will yields, it yields only because it consents to yield.

Our wills make us king of our own soul and master of our own destiny. To awaken to the fact that we have within us an unconquerable will that, if it will, may absolutely dominate our own lives is a step in becoming strong. We are strong. Each of us is strong. No matter how weak we feel, no matter how inadequate our strength may seem, no matter how great the obstacles before us—in fact, it does not matter about anything—we have within us a will that is the source of a strength that in our own lives and for our own purposes and for God's purpose is one of the mightiest things in the universe. To realize this is to realize that I can if I will. If I will use my will as it is capable of being used, if I will pour its strength into the channel of life, I shall be borne along by it to the desired goal. I shall accomplish what I will to accomplish. The reason so many people feel themselves so weak in spiritual things is that they do not realize that their will is the source of such wonderful strength and that they have within themselves the power to use that will as they may determine. I have said again and again in my writings, you can if you will, for nothing is more true.

For effective use my arm is just as strong as the amount of its strength that I use. The strength that is not used accomplishes nothing. So if we use only a part of the strength of our wills, we shall accomplish only a part of what we are capable of accomplishing. That reserve strength of will that has not been used has not profited us. It is there ready to use. The secret of being strong is using our wills as they are capable of being used. Many people never use a tenth of their will power. They drift along in supposed weakness. They count themselves weak, and counting themselves weak they feel weak, and have not the courage for great endeavor, while at the same time they have within themselves those very powers and qualities that rightly used would bring them to great strength and make possible great achievements.

Are you weak? It is only because you do not use your powers. The powers and capacities for great strength and accomplishment lie within you. Will you arouse yourself to what you really are, and then use your powers as God means you to?

There are other things that unite with our inherent capacity for strength to give us strength. In other words, there is a mental attitude that is favorable to the use of our strength. Isaiah sets forth this attitude saying, "In quietness and in confidence shall be your strength" (Isa. 30:15). Your strength lies in keeping quiet. You must not allow yourself to become agitated and bothered, nor to fear the consequences of what is before you. You must not be terrified by your adver-

saries if you will be strong. You must not allow
yourself to get all "worked up" over things. This
weakens you. Your strength is in quietness, in
facing whatever situation there is before you
with calmness, with your soul at rest, without
foreboding. What a wonderful picture the
prophet has drawn for us with a few bold strokes!
There is the Jewish nation threatened. Calamities
seem to be before them. They have need of all
the strength they can get. They need courage
and fortitude. They need help. But the prophet
says to them, "If you would be strong, just be
quiet. Do not get excited about things. Do not
get frightened." The Psalmist speaks in a similar
manner: "Be still, and know that I am God."
When trouble comes, keep calm; keep cool so
you can think and so you can act, so you can plan,
so you can summon your forces, and set them in
array where they are needed.

You will have small battles and great battles,
but just keep your quietness of soul. Just rest
serenely. Your trials will not be so hard to bear
if you keep quiet in them. You can meet opposi-
tion better when it comes if you will keep quiet.
The tongues of slander will not hurt you nearly
so much if you remain quiet. Things cannot take

hold upon you and "wear the very life out of you" if you keep quiet. In quietness shall be your strength.

There is another thing that goes along with quietness, and that is begotten by quiet self-control. That is confidence. The Apostle said, "I have written unto you, young men, because ye are strong." The confident courage of youth is a source of wonderful strength. God says to us, "Ye are strong." If we accept his word, that gives us confidence in the certainty of the outcome of our battles, if we fight. It assures us of victory. Doubting yourself is a source of weakness. The more you question, the more you fear. The more you shrink in timidity, the less of your strength you will use, and the easier you will fail. And yet, failure is unnecessary to you. Most victories are won or lost before the battle begins. "I can't" surrenders before the first gun is fired. "I can" charges the enemy at his first appearance, and scatters his legions in defeat. Many a young convert accomplishes things that some Christians of years' standing would shrink from attempting. The secret of this is that the young convert is strong through his confidence. He believes that God will give victory and he acts that way. Many times the one who has been longer in the way is weak because he has come to distrust himself. In many battles he has not used all his strength, and he has come to believe that what he has used is all the strength he possesses. He has not drawn upon his reserve strength. And so instead of getting stronger through the years he has become weaker—perhaps not weaker in reality, but in his feelings. He has the same strength of will, the same ability to use it, the same mighty inner force for accomplishment. But he has come to distrust himself, to question, to doubt, to fear; and so he does not believe he can do what he really could do if he would. He needs but the restoration of his confidence to be strong again, and to do exploits for the Lord. In quietness and confidence is our strength.

To be sure, we may be weak within ourselves, but God is our strength. A newspaper may be a weak thing. But we can wrap a stick of dynamite in it and it will be full of power. So we by nature may be very weak, but with God within us we are like the paper filled with dynamite—we have great capacity for accomplishing. Let us get busy and do what we are capable of doing. "Be strong in the Lord, and in the power of his might."

THE WORST THING IN THE WORLD

WHAT is the worst thing in the world? Some might say sickness, others poverty, others would say sin. But sickness and poverty can be endured without destroying one's happiness. Sin is a terrible thing, but there is an ever-available remedy for it, and one need not have it upon his conscience any longer than it takes him to submit to God and believe in him for pardon. There is another thing, however, that gets hold upon innocent souls, and, in fact, upon all sorts of people in all sorts of conditions. It brings dark clouds of gloom over them. It destroys their happiness. It drives away joy. It brings heaviness and distress. It has not one good thing about it. It has not one attractive quality. It has not one redeeming feature. It is bad, utterly bad. This evil thing is discouragement, and I do not think I err in calling it the worst thing in the world, for it robs all good things of their appearance of goodness when they come under its blighting touch and it adds an ever-increasing weight to every evil.

14

Many people have given up the struggle against sin and the attempt to serve God through discouragement. It has robbed them of their courage, hope, and energy. It has limited their activities. It has made them sit down and fold their hands, and with a voice of sorrow say, "It is no use to try. I cannot make a success. I am nothing but a failure. I just make one failure after another." Then what heaviness settles down over the soul, what a sense of hopeless defeat, what a feeling of weakness which in time may lead to despair!

There are only a few souls who have enough optimism to go along through life with never a feeling of discouragement. To most of us discouragement is not a stranger. It has come to sit beside us, and pour its doleful tale of woe into our ears on many occasions. It has cast dark shadows of gloom upon us. And I suppose we shall always be more or less subject to discouraging influences and their effects upon ourselves by our own actions. When discouragement comes it is so easy to increase it, and most of us are so prone to take the course that naturally increases it.

We do this in the first place by magnifying the difficulties, dangers, or evils that we have to meet in life. As we look at them and think over them they become enlarged. They fill our horizon more and more. We say within ourselves, "Oh, this duty is so hard. This difficulty is so great. This danger is so threatening. These evils are so inescapable." The more we look them over the worse they seem to become. The more we assert they are great the more they seem to increase. The more we look at them the more impossible it seems for us to surmount them and overcome them. People often magnify their troubles or their duties far beyond what they really are. This produces greater discouragement. As we continue to magnify these things our ability to meet them seems to decrease.

As we magnify our difficulties we naturally magnify our sense of weakness, our feeling of inability. The more we think about our weakness and inability, the less confidence we shall have in our ability, the less courage we shall have to attempt to do anything. And so this process goes on, alternately magnifying our difficulties, dangers, and duties, and minifying our own abilities. The farther we go in this process the darker things become, the more gloomy we feel. We become disheartened, and perhaps wish we had never been born.

If we have given way to discouragement or if we have not given way to it, but are fighting against it, there are certain steps to take that assuredly will bring us to victory. Discouragement can be overcome no matter how great it may be. No matter how long you have been in a discouraged condition, there is a way out. That way is one that you can take, which will lead you to success. The first thing to do is to take a square look at things. I do not mean to look at them through your feelings, but look at the facts just as though it were somebody else's case you were looking at. Look right at your difficulties; examine them carefully. Are they really as great as they seem? Are they as numerous as you suppose them to be? Are they really? Of course you feel they are. But dissect them. Get into their reality. Weigh them on a true balance, and be sure you keep your feelings off the scales. Take a look at your duties. Does God require more of you than he ought to require? Does he expect more of you than he will give you grace to do? Of course not. Are the things that threaten you as dangerous as they look? Get things sized up just as they are. Stop magnifying things. Stop thinking how great they are. They are not nearly so bad as they appear.

Now take a look at yourself. Are you really as weak as you feel? Is your inability as great as it seems? Are your failings and faults the full size they appear to be? Now really, have you not been magnifying these things? Have you not been counting yourself weaker than you really are if you would exert your strength? It is so easy to fold your hands and say, "It is no use to try," even when you have strength enough to rise up like a man or woman and overcome the things that confront you. So take a look at yourself. You are not nearly so weak as you feel. You can do a great many things that do not seem possible to you in your discouraged condition. Make an accounting of your assets. Think what you really can do if you try. Then take a look at God. See what a wonderful God you have. See the display of his power in the orderly processes of nature. The God whose voice sounds in the thunder, and whose footsteps shake the world, is a God who says to you, "I will help you."

What are the things that confront you? God's promises are true. He has said, "My grace is sufficient." Draw upon that grace. "Oh," you say, "if I just had grace," when there is a whole ocean of it to be had for the using. Begin to use your faith, to rouse your courage; get your will to succeed into action. Begin to assert within yourself that you can succeed. Look over the field of human beings that you know. Has anyone like you ever made a success? Has anyone like you ever risen above discouragement? Yes, thousands of such persons have. Well, what they have done you can do. Begin to assert that you are a child of the King, that God is your helper, that his strength is your strength, that no matter what circumstances you may face you and God can overcome them, that no matter what duties you may have God's grace will be given you to enable you to perform them. Begin to encourage yourself. Stop surrendering to your feelings. Be a man. Say, "I can and I will."

Look at the things you have to encourage you. Turn your eyes away from the dark side, look at the bright glow of God's grace. Believe his promises. Your feelings do not count. What matters it if you do feel discouraged? Thousands of other people have felt just that way. Their sky has been overcast and their lives gloomy. They have felt just as you have felt, that it was no use to try any more. Then they have taken hold of themselves, they have summoned their courage, they have gone at things like men and women, and their darkness has been dissipated. They have risen above all their troubles; they have put their feet upon their gloomy feelings, and they have triumphed in God. And so, discouraged soul, look away from the things that have discouraged you. Look at the things that will encourage and help you. And above all, put your trust in God and say, "I can and I will." To be sure, you will have some conflicts, but the road to victory is open before you, and by doing what you can yourself and by trusting in God for the help you need you can rise above your discouragement and know that you have overcome the worst thing in the world.

HE GOT USED TO IT

JOHN had not been saved so very long, but he was greatly enjoying his life. Salvation to him was the sweetest thing he had ever known. He abhorred sin. When he saw it or heard it in any form it was very obnoxious to him. He had a keen sense of its sinfulness. But after a while John went to work in a factory. There he was thrown into contact with men of all sorts, most of them given to profanity and obscenity. How he hated to hear such language! But hear it he must. His soul was vexed continually with it and he heartily wished himself in some other employment. But as time went on he did not seem to mind it so much, until finally he took it as a matter of course and paid little attention to it. One day a brother said to him, "John, how do you get along working with all those profane men?" "Oh," said John, "I've got used to it now. It doesn't bother me much any more."

Mary, John's wife, was saved in the meeting where John was saved. She, too, was very happy

in the Lord, but she lived in a neighborhood
where the people were much given to gossiping
about each other and where about all the women
discussed was each other, the scandals of the
neighborhood, fashions, and worldliness of various sorts. Mary had taken her part in this with
the others before she was saved, but after she
had found the Lord she abhorred it utterly. It
was very trying for her to listen to it any longer.
When her neighbors came in she tried to be
courteous to them and to listen to them somewhat from that standpoint, but she tried to turn
the conversation to spiritual things whenever
she could. She soon found, however, that her
neighbors did not care for such things. So little
by little she ceased to speak of them. After a
while she lost the keen sense of displeasure at
their conversation. Little by little, without her
being aware of it she became interested in the
things they talked about. After a while she began
to enjoy hearing the things of which they talked.
She was like John. Sin was not to her as it had
been. She had grown used to it.

But since John and Mary had become used to
sin, were they the same as before? In getting
used to these things had they lost anything them-

selves? Yes, they had lost something very real, something very vital to their souls. They did not have the same relish for the meetings that they formerly had. They did not have the same deep, abiding love for the church as individuals. They could see faults and shortcomings that they had not seen before in their brethren and sisters. They still prayed and testified in the prayer meetings. They still attended and enjoyed the preaching services, but there was not quite the same relish for the things of the Spirit. Their prayers were not so earnest as before. They were not so zealous for the salvation of the souls of the people as they had been. In getting to the place where sin was less sinful to them and less obnoxious to them they had come to where righteousness did not mean so much to them. In getting hardened to the sin about them they had also become hardened to righteousness.

Our love of righteousness and spiritual things is in direct proportion to our hatred for evil, and whenever we get used to evil so that it means little to us, righteousness also comes to mean less than it did to us. When the great gulf between sin and righteousness becomes filled up with indifference we almost lose sight of it. We need to be careful that we do not lose our sense of the sinfulness of sin.

It is natural for us to become used to whatever is about us. There is an adaptability to human nature through which we adjust ourselves to existing circumstances and conditions. If we are not careful this natural adaptability will take the edge off our sense of the sinfulness of sin, and as surely as that sense is blunted, something very vital to our spiritual prosperity has been lost. Lot lived in Sodom and remained a righteous man, but he did so only because he kept his soul in an attitude toward God where he was continually vexed by the deeds of the unrighteous. He never lost his sense of the sinfulness of sin, and that was the one thing that protected him among the evil people with whom he was surrounded.

The closer we live to God the more we will hate evil; and the truly spiritual person can never find pleasure in any form of sin no matter who it is that is guilty of the sin. God never gets used to sin. If we retain our godlikeness we can never become used to it. Therefore, if we begin to feel less concerned about the wickedness of those about us, if we realize we are becoming indifferent to it, if we can hear the name of God taken in vain or hear obscene stories and not have our soul roused in indignation against them, we should be warned that we are drifting away from that high plane of spirituality on which it is our privilege and duty to live.

There is also another side to this question. People come to realize that they are not spiritual as they once were. They realize that they are not living so close to God as they did in the past. Perhaps they feel it keenly at first and make efforts to recover what they have lost; but not making earnest enough efforts or not being diligent enough, they do not recover the lost ground. They go on realizing they are less spiritual than they should be, and if they continue in this condition they will presently get used to it. They will have a realization of it perhaps when they compare themselves with what they were; but there comes a sort of indifference, a sort of adjusting oneself to the conditions, and after a while they are very hard to move to any attempt to regain their lost spirituality. They have become used to being unspiritual. They are not just altogether satisfied with it, but they would rather be as they are than to make an effort to be more spiritual. So they drift along. Oh, of course, they would like to be more spiritual like the brethren, but they have become used to being as they now are and as they are doing pretty well, why bother about things? To be sure, they have lost their former zeal, but they have got used to being without it. They used to feel very keenly when they omitted duties, but now they have become used to omitting them and it does not bother them so much.

We can get into a place where it is just natural for us to love righteousness and to hate iniquity, to love to do all we can for God and not hold back from effort. We can get used to service and sacrifice, and this we must do if we are to prosper in our souls as God designs that we should prosper, but woe unto us if we sacrifice those qualities of righteousness in the soul that we must sacrifice to get used to sin.

THE IMAGE IN THE MIRROR

THE mirror is a very common object in all civilized countries. We have all seen our images in mirrors; also we have seen the images of other persons and objects. We have observed two things about these images. First, that there must be an object to be mirrored or there will be no image in the mirror. Second, that the image we see in the mirror may be a perfect or an imperfect image of the object mirrored. The perfection with which the object is mirrored depends to a large extent upon the quality of the mirror. We have a mirror which was long exposed to the sunshine. The quicksilver on the back of the glass was affected by the sunlight and now the image, instead of being clear and well defined, is indistinct.

Other mirrors distort the image and make it appear very different in size, shape, or outline from what the object really is. The character of the mirror, therefore, is highly important; especially so when it comes to our spiritual mirror. Do you ask what is our spiritual mirror? Our minds are our spiritual mirrors. We cannot see God, but we have in our minds the mental reflection of him. His image stands out there, and instead of viewing him we view that image; so the picture of God that we have in our minds is to us the real God. Our eyes cannot pierce to heaven and behold him on his throne. We can only form a mental picture of him. Paul speaks of this, saying, "Beholding as in a mirror the glory of the Lord" (II Cor. 3:18, A. R. V.).

God works in us and all about us. His working is mirrored in our minds. The mental picture of God which we have has great effects on our attitude toward him and our relations with him. Any wrong idea of God produces a distorted image of him, and if we draw our conclusion of what he really is from that distorted image, it is sure powerfully to affect our minds and our relation and attitude toward him. It is important, therefore, that we have correct ideas of God. We see varied ideas of God and Christ reflected in the New Testament as they appeared in the minds of the people. Some said of Christ, "He is a good man." The image in their mental mirror showed him in this character. Others said, "He deceiveth the people." When they looked into their mirror they saw a deceiver.

One writer of the Bible saw him as one altogether lovely, the fairest of ten thousand. Others saw him as one to be dreaded, and they were terrified because of him.

In one of the parables the servant said of his Lord, "Thou art an austere man." His idea was of a severe Master, strict and exacting. No wonder he said, "I was afraid." There are many people who have just such ideas of God now. They feel he is strict, that he will bring them to account in an arbitrary manner. Their image of God, reflected in their mind, has little of mercy, kindness, goodness, or similar qualities. It emphasizes his justice, his abhorrence of evil, and his strictness. Now a person having that idea of God can never draw near to him. He may fear him. He may shrink in terror from the thought of dying and going into his presence, he may try to do what pleases him from a sense of fear, but he never can love him as can those who have a truer picture of God in their minds.

We can misjudge God as easily as we misjudge people. In my early Christian experience I met a minister who looked very stern. For a few days

I was thrown closely in his company. I was in bondage all the time. I was afraid of him. I thought his piercing eyes looked right through me. I almost trembled when I came near him, but after a little longer association I began to feel that I had misjudged him. I found that instead of being stern and critical he was very tender and kindhearted; and later he was like a father to me. I could then come to him with my problems. I could feel easy in his presence. I could enjoy his society, where before I was tortured by his presence. Now, a wrong idea of God has exactly this effect. It makes our relations with him unpleasant. It makes us fear and tremble. But when we come to know the tender father heart, the compassionate love, the mercy that endureth forever, we can then approach him with confidence; we can be easy before him, and can open our hearts to him. But, ah, dear soul, if the mirror into which you are looking shows God as an "austere man," remember the trouble is in the mirror, not in God. Learn about him, get him properly reflected in your mind. Get rid of your wrong idea concerning him. Know him as he is.

Some people think that God has no time for

them and no particular interest in them except
when they sin. They seem to feel that he is
hunting for faults in them all the time. Their
life is made a life of bondage by this wrong idea
of God. God knew when he made us finite beings
that we would have faults, and his interest in
us is not so much to look for our faults as to
help us. Does the mother look for faults in her
child? or does her love make her overlook the
faults that others see? God's love is tender as
a mother's. Therefore, it is not our faults for
which he is looking. He sees them, to be sure, and
desires us to correct them, but our faults do not
keep him from loving us. And he has time for us.
He is interested in our welfare. Sometimes when
we have faltered and failed it seems we cannot
help but feel that God must get discouraged
with us, and that he grows impatient with us,
and that it is of no use for us to try any more.
This is not true. It is a distorted image of God
at which we are looking. God is not like that
image at all. If we are viewing God as being
harsh, critical, austere, and without interest in
us, let us ask him to change the mirror in our
minds and give us a real view of himself that
shows him as he is.

You can find his image in the Bible. It reflects him correctly. It shows him as he is. Where your idea or mine is not in harmony with his reflection in the Bible we should take the reflection in the Bible and reject that in our minds. Look at his image in the Bible. It pictures him as being a God of love. Look at his image in Isaiah 54:10, "For the mountains shall depart, and the hills be removed; but my kindness shall not depart from thee, neither shall the covenant of my peace be removed, saith the Lord that hath mercy on thee." Troubled heart, look upon this image. Look upon it until it is reflected in your heart. Look upon it till you come to believe this is God's real image, your God's image.

IF YOU WERE IN GOD'S PLACE

IT IS very natural for us to think what we would do if we were in someone else's place. Often we hear people say, "If I were in his place I would do so and so." Sometimes we even think what we would do if we were in God's place. Sometimes we are tempted to judge God and think that if we were in his place we would do differently from what he does. I suppose it is natural to think thus, for we do not have the wisdom that God has, and therefore we do not see things as he sees them. Sometimes we can put ourselves in the place of others in our thoughts and determine what properly ought to be done under such conditions. Sometimes we can determine what God ought to do under such a condition. He has revealed to us enough of his nature and of the principles on which he acts so that we can determine how he ought to act and how he will act under certain conditions. Of course, many times we cannot determine what is wisest and best;

and if he were to give us the power to act in his place, we should not act nearly so wisely nor so well as he does.

We are sometimes inclined to misjudge God's attitude toward us. Very often this is because we hold the wrong attitude toward ourselves. There are people who are constantly finding fault with themselves and condemning themselves. Sometimes this is not done in sincerity, for if anyone else should say about such a person what he says of himself he would be greatly hurt or offended. In such a case it proves the insincerity of the one who speaks slightingly of himself. Such persons do not really believe they are what they pretend to be or that they have the shortcomings and weaknesses and faults they accuse themselves of having.

There are others, however, who are sincere in their judgment of themselves, but they are harsher in their judgment of themselves than they are in their judgment of others. Some dear conscientious souls are always heaping self-condemnation on themselves. They are always judging themselves by a higher and more exacting standard than they judge anyone else. They have not a proper degree of confidence in them-

selves. Of course, there are those who go to
the other extreme and who excuse in themselves
what they would not excuse in others. There
are those who pass over things in themselves
that they, even in their hearts, know are not
right. They go on professing to be all right when
they know they are not, and when they know
they are guilty of misconduct. Of this class I
shall not speak here, but of the opposite class
who are visiting heavy judgments upon themselves all the time, those who are being unjust to
themselves.

There are many such. They have a feeling
that someway, somehow, God requires of them
more than he does of others, that he judges
them by a standard different from that by which
he judges others, that he will not excuse in them
what he excuses in others. It is unfair thus to
treat ourselves. Let us put ourselves in God's
place. Would we judge someone if we were God
and they were in our present situation; would
we judge them just as we judge ourselves? If
we were as good and kind and merciful and
forbearing and long-suffering as we know God to
be, what kind of attitude would we hold toward
one who has the same desires that we have? If

we have a sincere desire to please God, does he
not know it, does he not respect this desire, does
he not take it into consideration in judging us?
If our purpose is to serve him according to the
truth, if it is the deep, settled intent of our hearts
to do what pleases him, and we were in God's
place and could look down upon that purpose
in the heart of someone even if that person were
coming short of his purposes in some respects,
even if he were not carrying out his full intent
because of weakness or through force of circumstances, or through other things he could not
control, would we judge him as harshly as we
are judging ourselves? Looking down upon a
heart filled with the same longings as are in your
heart, a heart having the same hopes, passing
through the same struggles, having the same
disappointments, realizing the possession of the
same faults and shortcomings, would we hold
just the attitude toward some other person in
that situation that we hold toward ourselves?
Would we not rather be more merciful to them
than we are to self? Would we not rather consider
the earnest endeavor, the sincere desire of that
soul? Would we not see the grief that its faults

caused, and the heartaches that resulted from the realization of shortcomings?

Do we think and feel that God condemns us, yet when we think of another in that situation we feel rather like pitying and being merciful and excusing? Are we more just and merciful than God is? Are we kinder than God? Have we more long-suffering than he has? Have we more tender compassionate love for a soul than he, a deeper sympathy, a greater readiness to show mercy? Ah, do not judge God by condemning yourself. Show the mercy to yourself that you, in God's stead, would show to another in your situation. If you know your heart is sincere toward God, if you are striving to serve him, yet all the time are condemning yourself, finding fault with yourself, heaping reproaches upon yourself, and then when you think of it you realize that you would not feel toward one in your situation and circumstances as you feel toward yourself if you were in God's place, or even when you are in your own place, then you are judging yourself harshly. You are wronging yourself. You are heaping condemnation upon yourself that you should not.

It is the most conscientious souls who thus

wrong themselves. Be just to yourself. Judge yourself righteously. Show the same mercy to yourself that you would show to another. Do not have a higher standard for yourself than you have for others. God has the same standard for all. God expects some imperfections in us. He expects us to serve him with all our hearts. He expects us to be obedient to his Word and to the guidance of his Holy Spirit, but he does not expect in us the same perfection that is in himself. We can never be as wise or as strong or as able to surmount obstacles successfully as he.

IS YOUR HEART FIXED?

DAVID once wrote, "My heart is fixed, O God, my heart is fixed" (Ps. 57:7). The word, "fixed" is used in two different senses. Sometimes it is incorrectly given the meaning of "repaired." I once heard a man read the above text and then remark, "There are many people today whose hearts need fixing." It is true there are many hearts in a very bad condition, but it is not repairing that they need. The old heart needs to be replaced by a new one, for when sin has done its work in the heart it is past repairing. The Lord said, "A new heart will I give you."

So the Psalmist did not mean that his heart was repaired, but he used the word "fixed" in a different signification. To fix a thing in place means to fasten it there. When our hearts are fixed in the sense of the text quoted, they are established, settled, rooted, and grounded in God. They are decided, set, unwavering. In that sense God desires all our hearts to be fixed. It is not his purpose that we be unsettled, or doubtful, that we be like people walking in a fog, or that we be harassed by uncertainties. He does not want us to be wavering and fearing. He desires us to plant our feet firmly upon the truth, to know it is the truth and to be definitely decided as to the course of our lives.

In the first place, he desires our minds to be fixed concerning himself. He wishes us to know just what he is, his purpose, his attitude toward us, the relation he is willing to sustain to us, and the help he is willing to give us. Of the righteous it is said, "His heart is fixed, trusting in the Lord" (Ps. 112:7). God wishes us to be certain of the fact that we can repose the utmost confidence in his upholding promises with an assurance of mind and a rest of soul that is not disturbed. He desires us to trust in him unquestioningly, to feel that he is absolutely true, that we may rely upon him to help us, and that he will never fail us. We should no more question his goodness, kindness, and his care for us and his absolute faithfulness to us than we would question his greatness or his creative power. There is no more reason to question God in any way or to doubt him or to fear that perhaps he may fail us than there is to fear the solid earth beneath our feet will sink into a yawning abyss and let us perish. O brother and sister, get your heart so fixed on God, your confidence in him so established, your trust in him so unwavering that his love, his faithfulness and kindness and fatherhood, will be so real to you that it will be just as much a fact to you as any fact. You need not be afraid to trust God. Heaven and earth shall pass away, but his word shall never pass away. His promises are a solid rock beneath your feet. Let your confidence run to God until you can exclaim, "My heart is fixed, I will trust in the living God!"

Then too, our hearts need to be fixed in the faith. There are gods many and faiths many. There is a multitude of voices saying, "Lo here, lo there," and if our hearts are to be fixed in this age when there are so many fads in doctrine, we must get settled firmly in the truth. But can we really know the truth? Yes. Jesus said, "Ye shall know the truth, and the truth shall make you free." We can get beyond the questioning of the doubted and the scoffing of the scoffer; we can get beyond the criticism of the critic, and reach the place where we know for ourselves the truth of God. There will be, of course, many problems which we cannot solve and many questions which we cannot answer, but it is our privilege to search the Bible and to commune with God until none of these false doctrines scattered abroad will cause us to waver, to question, or to fear. There is only one doctrine which is according to godliness; there is only one doctrine which satisfies the soul, because there is only one doctrine which is the truth and that one doctrine brings us to God and brings our souls into the haven of his will; and when we have once anchored there the stormy winds of doctrine may lash the sea till its waves roar, but our hearts may be calmly content and at rest.

Then our hearts need to be fixed in purpose. It is not enough to believe in God and to believe in his truth. The devils believe that and their faith only torments them. We may believe in many things and yet be wavering, tossed to and fro, uncertain and unsatisfied. To get out of this condition we must adopt a fixed purpose of adjusting ourselves to the truth, of obeying God, of living for him every day. Some look forward to the future with uncertainty. They are never certain as to how they are going to do tomorrow. They mean to be true, but they are rather doubtful whether they always will be true. This uncertainty is based upon a lack of fixed purpose to be true and a determination always to trust God for sufficient grace. We should press on beyond that realm of wavering purpose: settle the matter once for all that you are always going to be true; that you are always going to do the right thing; that you are always going to have sufficient grace, because you are always going to seek it. Then you can say, "My heart is fixed, my purpose is established." Then you will be on solid ground.

Our hearts need to be fixed in our love toward God. Our affections should be definitely set upon things above, and not allowed to run after worldly things. It is this lack of fixity of love that permits self to come to love the things of the world which are enmity against God and ruinous to the soul. If we get our love once fixed on God our hearts riveted to his heart with warm affection, we can say as did Paul, "Who shall separate us from the love of Christ?"

One thing to remember is that though our hearts are fixed, settled and established, there can be no fixity of our emotions. They will rise and fall like the tides of the sea. We shall feel good; we shall feel bad; we shall feel joyful, and we shall feel sorrowful. We shall feel zealous, and sometimes we shall feel careless. But these emotions with all their changeableness should never be allowed to affect the fixity of our hearts. There should be no fluctuation of purpose. Our faces should be ever toward the goal, and whether our footsteps be light and joyous or whether they be heavy with weariness, we should keep an unflagging purpose ever to press on.

There may be a variation of our consecration, and it may reach to the mark, to the fullness of God's requirements, but if we are not careful our consecration and devotion will fluctuate, and we will find ourselves growing less devoted and less consciously all the Lord's. There is need, therefore, that our hearts shall be fixed in consecration and kept up to the full standard.

We may say to the Lord, "My heart is fixed," and our voice may be the voice of joy, or the voice of sorrow. We may be facing difficulty or danger, or we may be speaking with the confidence of prosperity. But whatever the note in our voice, let us constantly speak with that determination which embodies the strength of our soul, "My heart is fixed, trusting in the Lord. He will be my sufficiency and I will be his faithful child."

WHEN GOD CHASTISES

NO ONE likes to be chastised. Any child would rather be petted than punished. The children of God are no exception to this rule. But as discipline is needed in the life of the child, so it is needed in the life of the Christian. The child who disciplines himself sufficiently does not need very much parental discipline; so the Christian who properly disciplines himself may not need God's discipline. But who among us properly disciplines himself in every avenue of life? All of us have imperfections, and I suppose all of us are blameworthy at various times and to various degrees. Therefore we are told that God "scourgeth every son whom he receiveth." Again it speaks of "chastisement, whereof all are partakers."

It is, therefore, the common lot of Christians to receive chastisement from the Lord. This chastisement may come as direct reproofs from the Spirit, and these are sometimes sharp and stern. Sometimes they are tender and appealing.

However they may come from the Spirit, we should not allow ourselves to be crushed nor discouraged by them, for God "dealeth with you as with sons." We are shown in various places how God sometimes uses men to scourge people; and again circumstances, failures, disappointed expectations, slights, losses, mistreatment, and scores of other things are used by God to work out that discipline which is necessary for our souls.

His purpose is to correct us, to instruct us, and to make us partakers of his holiness. God does not find pleasure in chastising us. He does not do it merely as a punishment. He does it as a discipline, having in view an outcome that is desirable to him and profitable to us. Though God disciplines in love, we must not expect to receive his chastisement without feeling its effects. No chastisement, Paul tells us, is joyous for the present. We may expect to suffer when God chastises us. Sometimes he may take away from us something very much desired, just as the parent must deprive his child of some pleasure for his good, that he may be profited and be more greatly blessed in some other way.

The problem of the parent is to bring the

child up in the way that it should go, to develop in it a character such as it needs for its future life. God's problem with us is the same. Much must be left unsaid, but one thing we should keep in mind: the fact that he chastises us does not prove that we are not holding a proper attitude of service and submission toward him. His chastisement proves we are his sons; so we should not be cast down nor disquieted. We should receive his chastisement with submission. In Job 34:31-32 we have some very good advice as to how we shall do when the Lord chastises us. Let us notice this scripture carefully: "Surely it is meet to be said unto God, I have borne chastisement." "I have borne chastisement"; that is, I have submitted to it. I have not rebelled against thee. I have not murmured or complained. I have not grieved or lamented. I have not grown stubborn or self-willed.

This is the attitude we should adopt at such times. The speaker in Job recognized that it was God's hand that had smitten; therefore, he did not resent it. We are told to humble ourselves under the mighty hand of God. How often people resist God's chastising! Sometimes they complain and murmur. Sometimes they accuse God and accuse themselves. Sometimes they rebel. Sometimes they become sullen, and resent it as some children resent punishment. Such children miss the good that would be in the discipline for them if they met it properly and submitted themselves to it. We must meet God's discipline with humble hearts, uncomplainingly, unresistingly, recognizing that it is his hand of love that chastens. Sometimes we forget that back of circumstances is God. We are too prone to separate God in our thoughts from the things that happen to us in life. Many of his chastisements are not recognized when they come. His hand is not seen in them. We take it for granted that things just happened that way, when often God made them happen thus for our good and for his glory. Instead of being cast down and lamenting or being discouraged, we should look back of the circumstances or back of the words of reproof and see the tender heart that prompts it and the faithful love that has smitten us. Then we should bow in humble submission and endure chastening as a loving son. This is often the test of our life and of the sincerity of our submission.

After we have reached the place where we can say, "I have borne chastisement," what is proper for us to say next? What attitude shall we adopt? Listen to the words of the scripture, "I have borne chastisement, I will not offend any more" (A. R. V.). I will not offend any more. Here is the purpose to be obedient. Here is the determination that the future conduct shall be superior to the past. If God's chastisement does not bring the soul into this attitude it has failed in its purpose, and the soul that adopts any other attitude is doing injury and injustice to himself and to God. Paul reproved the Corinthian church. When he wrote them again he exclaimed, "What clearing of yourselves!" They had taken his reproof to heart. They had profited by it. They had adopted a better course. Now he can rejoice in them. So when we say to the Lord, in our chastisement, "I will not offend any more," we have adopted the very attitude that he purposed for us to adopt, an attitude which will be a blessing to our soul.

There is something else that follows too. "That which I see not teach thou me." That is, instruct me that I may more fully follow thy will. Reveal to me how I may live closer to thee and more worthily before thee; how my obedience may be more full and my service more acceptable. I need thy instruction. I open my heart to thee. Reveal to me thy truth. This implies not only a willingness to be instructed, but a willingness to be obedient and a heart responsive to the revealed will.

A SURE CURE FOR HEART TROUBLE

HEART trouble is a serious and highly unpleasant thing. We always feel sympathy for people who are so afflicted. Trouble with the natural heart, however, is not nearly so serious nor does it cause such distress as spiritual heart trouble. There are two kinds of natural heart trouble: one is organic, the other sympathetic or nervous heart trouble. The first is a diseased condition of the heart. The second is a reaction from something else.

So in the spiritual life there are two kinds of heart trouble. One comes from sin in the heart. In other words, it is organic heart trouble. The other is trouble that does not arise from sin, but is caused by something else. However, great suffering may come from either of these. But I am glad to tell you that I have found a specific, a sure cure for heart trouble of every kind that afflicts the spiritual man.

We are told that man is born unto trouble, and that his days are full of trouble, and most of us

51

know this to be true by personal experience. We shall always have trouble, but all persons are not affected in the same way by their troubles. Trouble takes greater hold upon some people than upon others. Some have a way of meeting trouble and conquering it so that it does not affect their soul-life adversely. Others are continually troubled and bothered. They do not seem to be at rest. They have little peace. They are often distressed. In other words, they have frequent attacks of heart trouble. The trouble gets hold of their hearts. It not only perplexes them and tries them, but it hinders them in their Christian life. Often they look careworn and troubled. Their countenance is a mirror of their heart. If they would tell what is in their hearts, they would be continually pouring out a tale of woe.

God meant for his people to be happy; not happy because they had no troubles, but happy in spite of them. When people realize that they are afflicted with natural heart trouble they usually go to the doctor and get a bottle of medicine. When we have spiritual heart troubles we ought to go to the Great Physician and get a remedy for our heart trouble. Earthly physicians are often unable to cure heart trouble, but the Great Physician has a remedy that has never yet failed when properly used. It is a cure-all in the truest sense. There is no ill of the human heart that it cannot reach and overcome. Have you spiritual heart trouble? Why do you not take God's remedy? No matter what your heart's trouble nor how much distress it has brought you, God has a remedy that will be effectual in giving you not only immediate relief, but complete healing, and the fullest restoration if you will take it according to directions. The greatest trouble physicians have is to get their patients to take their medicine according to directions. The Great Physician has the same trouble. People want to be cured, but they do not want to take his remedy as he prescribes it. They cannot be cured if they will not follow directions, but he guarantees a cure if they will be obedient and follow directions.

Do you wish to be cured of your heart trouble, whatever it is? God's prescription was brought down from heaven nearly two thousand years ago. You have had it in your house this long time. Do you know what it is? As already stated, it will work a perfect cure. So take it for your troubled heart, and be at rest.

This great prescription is found in John 14:1. Here Jesus says, "Let not your heart be troubled." It shows that heart trouble is not necessary. It also shows that the responsibility for our having heart trouble rests upon us. He says, "Let not your heart be troubled," and that certainly signifies that we have the power to prevent heart trouble. According to Jesus, then, believing in God is a complete cure for all heart trouble. We may have many troubles in life. We may meet disappointments, losses, cares; friends may prove untrue, and a thousand other things may arise to trouble us; but if we truly believe in God it will prevent these things from causing the trouble to get into our hearts in a way that affects our Christian lives and hinders us in our service to God or to humanity.

Believing in God in the sense that provides a remedy for our troubles means relying on him, taking his promises to be our very own, taking them as realities—realities to serve us just as practically and effectively as our hands or our eyes serve us. That is what his promises were meant to be to us.

Just believe in God. That is the remedy for your heart trouble. His promises will be fulfilled. He will take you through though waves of trouble roll around you; and he will keep your heart in peace in the midst of the wildest storm or the greatest difficulty, and under the most unfavorable circumstances. But to be cured of your heart trouble you must take his remedy—believe in God.

WHY WE SHOULD NOT FEAR

WE ARE in a world full of dangers. Perils throng about us on every side. We are in peril from disease germs, from poison, from accidents, from evil persons, from the forces of nature. There are so many things about us calculated, when circumstances are favorable, to destroy our life, our health, our happiness. A thousand dangers surround us on every hand. In the spiritual realm there is a continued conflict. It is useless to cry "Peace, peace," for we are surrounded by the forces of evil.

In the midst of this evil is it any wonder that we should fear? Why should we not be afraid? What assurance have we of the safety of body or soul? What wonder if we shrink back from the conflicts, the trials, and the dangers of life? But God calmly looks down upon it all, sees it all, and yet says again and again to us, "Fear not," "Be not afraid," "Let not your hearts be troubled"; and Paul says, "In nothing terrified by your adversaries." How can we help being afraid? Why should not terror take hold upon us? Why should we not shrink in dismay?

Well, there are plenty of reasons why we should not. God enumerates in Isaiah 43 some of these reasons why we should not fear. There he says to his people, "O Israel, Fear not." He does not say this merely to make them overlook the dangers about them or to give them a false sense of security. He says this because they really have no reason to be afraid. In summing up the reasons why they should not be afraid, he gives the following: he calls himself "the Lord that created thee." God created us as we are. He put us in the midst of all these dangers. We are weak because we are finite humans. God created us thus, and the fact that he created us thus places upon him a responsibility with regard to us. If he places us in the midst of these temptations, trials, difficulties, and dangers, will he not be responsible for the outcome? And if he is responsible for the outcome is he not responsible to see that conditions are such that we can meet these difficulties victoriously? Is he not under obligation to provide for our safety? Certainly he is. More than that, he will not shrink from the obligation that rests upon him to provide for us.

Again he says he is "he that formed thee."
God not only created the race of mankind, but
his divine power operates in every life. The individual is the product of the operation of forces
that had their origin in God. He is, therefore,
responsible for the individual as well as for the
race. He will not shrink from this responsibility.

Another reason he gives why we should not
fear is, "For I have redeemed thee." There are
not only those natural sources of danger about
us, but we have greatly endangered our souls
for time and eternity by doing evil in the sight
of the Lord. We have permitted sin to come into
our hearts. We have let it destroy our peace
and happiness. We have let it work wrath within
us. We are responsible for the dangers of our
souls that we bring upon ourselves. But to those
who have become his people he says, "Fear not:
for I have redeemed thee." The power of sinful
habit has been broken. The power of iniquity
that continually endangered us has been swept
away. He has made us free. He gave his only begotten Son to die for us. He paid a price greater
than we can estimate, for our redemption. He has
purchased us, redeemed us from the power of sin.
He gives this as one of the reasons why we should

not fear. And it is an excellent reason, for since
he has paid such a price for us he will show a
regard for us worthy of that price. Our welfare
means much to him on this account.

Again he says, "I have called thee by thy
name." That means he has given individual attention to us. He is individually concerned with
our welfare. That feeling of individual con-
cern for us will naturally prompt him to take
such steps and provide such safeguards as will
work out for our safety. He gave Israel his name;
so he has given you and me a new name, a secret
name. To whom do men give names? They give
names to their sons, to those who are near and
dear to them. So when God gave to us our
new name and wrote it down in the book of life
he pledged himself to look out for our interests
as a father looks out for the interests of his son.
He accepted the full measure of responsibility
that was his. He will not come short of fulfilling
that responsibility to the utmost.

He emphasizes this point by saying, "Thou art
mine." We naturally take care of that which is
ours. It has a special value to us that the things
belonging to other people do not have. We are
interested more in those things that belong to us

than we are in those things that belong to others.
This is perfectly natural. It is likewise natural
for God to be interested in the things that belong
to him. He is interested in guarding us against
the assaults of the evil one; so he warns us of the
places of danger, of the things that are dangerous.
He points out the way of safety and says, "Walk
therein."

He gives still another reason why we should
not fear. "Thou hast been precious in my sight"
(vs. 4, A. R. V.). Why are we more careful with
our pocketbooks than we are with an almanac?
Why do people build great steel safes and great
vaults of steel and concrete? They do not put
their hats and shoes and pocketknives in such
places when they are built. They put their treas-
ures therein, and they put them there for safety.
Why is a lady so concerned about the safety of
her jewels. They are precious in her sight. We are
God's jewels. We are precious in his sight; therefore, he will take the best possible care of us.
He will guard us securely, but he gives still another reason why we should not fear. "I have
loved thee." Now, there is no greater reason than
this. What will we not do for the safety of our
loved ones? When they are in danger what pangs

of fear go through us, piercing us like darts! How forgetful of self we are at such times! What dangers we will brave! We have but to know that our loved ones are in danger to do everything possible for their safety. God loves us; therefore, he says, "Fear not." That love is our safeguard. That love is our strength. All the strength of that love, which means all the strength of God, is at our command. Not a moment shall we be without divine help.

He gives us still another reason for not being afraid, saying, "I am with thee." We might fear were we alone. We might shrink if we must provide for our own safety. But he says, "I am with thee." And here is a further promise, "Lo, I am with you alway, even unto the end of the world." Not a moment shall we be left alone. Not a moment shall we be without divine help. Not a moment shall we be without His care.

HOW OLD WAS METHUSELAH?

ONE of the first things that I remember having learned in Sunday school was that Methuselah was the oldest man. I learned that he lived, according to the record, longer than anyone else in the history of the world whose age is given. The Bible puts his age at nine hundred and sixty-nine years. I am not going to contradict the Bible, yet I have come to believe that Methuselah was not the oldest man. Oh, yes, he was the oldest, so far as days and years go, but days and years are only one way of measuring the length of life. Measured thus, Methuselah's life was exceedingly long. But this is a rather uncertain standard of measurement. It does not tell us much. We must have another standard to tell the real length of a man's life. The best standard I know by which to measure life is by what is accomplished in it. There is a great difference between mere existence and real living. A man may eat and sleep, walk about, talk, and do a variety of things three hundred and sixty-five days in a year, and perhaps live only five days of that time a life that really counts. He has existed three hundred and sixty days and lived five days. In those five days he has done something worth while. He has done something worth putting in the records. He has done something that really added to the sum of his life. The rest of the year was lived about as an animal lives. That man, when his life is summed up, only lived five days in that year, and so if we add up all his days that he really lived, we may find that his life was very short after all, though measured in years it may have been quite long.

Now, we have reason to believe that something of this sort was true of Methuselah. Here is his life's record. He was born; he married; he brought up a family; he died. There was nothing else in his life worth putting into the record. Forty-six words tell the story of his life. Thirty-five of these words tell about his age; all the rest that is said of him requires only eleven words, and when a man's life can be told in eleven words it does not seem, when judged by accomplishments, that he has lived very long. Of course much can be said in a few words sometimes, but

not much is said in these few words. So I conclude that in real accomplishment, in the things
that are really worth while, in years that were
real living, as far as the record goes, Methuselah
was a rather short-lived man. That long stretch
of years seems barren indeed.

I have frequently walked through cemeteries
and read the inscriptions on the tombstones. On
many of them we see the legend, born— died—
aged—. Some of those people had lived many
years while others' lives had been cut short; but
I wondered, if we knew the real story of their
age, if we knew the sum of all the days in their
lives that really amounted to anything, what
their age would truly be. Some men live a long
time in a little while; others live only a little in
a long time. The head of John the Baptist was
cut off when he was less than thirty-five years
old, yet John the Baptist had accomplished more
than all the prophets before him. Jesus Christ
was crucified when he was not yet thirty-five,
but what amazing things he accomplished in
those few short years.

The value of life is not reckoned by its length
but by its accomplishments. There should be a
purpose in every day of life, a purpose for the

whole life and a purpose for each day of the life. A life without a purpose can never be a full life. It is not living, it is merely existing. The person without a definite purpose in life is like a ship without a rudder. Such living is mere drifting, not steering. Such a person is the plaything of circumstances. The ship drifts in whichever direction the wind is blowing. So a life without a purpose drifts, drifts.

We should put something of value into every day of our life. If we ourselves do not put something into our lives, they will contain nothing. We once constructed a cistern. We had it built very carefully. We desired that it be a very good one so that we might drink the water. A short time after it was constructed a heavy rain fell and soaked up the ground thoroughly, but there was no water in the cistern. It was a good cistern, therefore no water could soak in through its walls, but it was an empty cistern. It had capacity, but no contents. Plenty of water had fallen on the roof to have filled it full, but there was no water in the cistern. It is that way with many lives. There are many things to be accomplished all about them. There are many things that might enrich them and beautify them and make them worth while, but though there are opportunities all about them, though there are many things that might fill their lives, still their lives are empty. The reason the cistern was empty was because there was nothing as yet to conduct the water to it. The rain that fell did not go into the cistern, and so there are many lives that are empty while there are opportunities of usefulness all about the person.

So many are ready to say, "Oh, my life does not count. I cannot do anything worth while." As long as one believes that, one's life will be empty. God never created a single human being to live a useless life. He has given everyone the capacity to do things, to fill his life with worthwhile things, with accomplishments that really count; and you, my reader, are one of those to whom God not only gave the power to do something, but upon whom he lays the responsibility of doing something. He expects you not to be like a broken cistern that can hold no water, or like a cistern that has no inlet, but he expects you to fill your life with endeavor. He expects you to have a purpose in your life. He expects you to have a goal toward which you are pressing forward each day. He is ready and willing to help you. He will plan your life for you. He will help you put that plan into execution, but you must not say, "I can't." You can do what God wants you to do. You can be what God wants you to be. Your life can be a worth-while life in your situation and in your circumstances. If it is not so it is because you are not making use of your opportunity. It is because you are merely drifting. Perhaps you are folding your hands and saying, "I can't; I can't." That is the coward's plea. That is what the person who is unwilling says. That is the evidence of faithlessness. Recently someone wrote me saying, "What is the use for me to try when it is predestinated that I can never be anything or do anything?" Such talk comes from discouragement, or is mere nonsense. In either case it is untrue. God means for our lives to be worth while. When we come to close our eyes in death we should be able to look back over our lives and see that something real has been put into every day, something of value that will count for eternity.

But it is not the showy things that are real accomplishments. Perhaps we can never do anything that will be written in history. Perhaps men will not applaud us or even take note of our lives, but God will take note. If we put into each day faithfulness, real service to God, kindness, hopefulness, and take advantage of whatever opportunities of service and of self-improvement that come to us, every day will be worth while. Every day will add to the sum total of our lives.

Methuselah lived nearly three times as long as Enoch, but of Enoch it is said that he "walked with God . . . . three hundred years." That is a record of real accomplishment. That is a record perhaps never excelled. If you and I make as good a record, if it may be written of us that we walked with God, our lives will have been worth while. So if you will do this one thing, if you will walk with God, you need not trouble yourself about doing great things or about getting a great name, for you will be doing the greatest of all things and getting a name more enduring than could come from any other accomplishment. But live every day in God's way, and every day will be a day of real life to you and a permanent addition to the record of your life.

THE SHOT THAT MISSED

AN ARCHERY contest was in progress. One after another the contestants stepped up to the line, took careful aim, and let fly their arrows at the target. Arrow after arrow embedded its point in the target, some near its center, others farther away. Finally one of the contestants who was waiting his turn stepped up to the mark, poised his arrow carefully upon the string of his bow, and with a look of confidence on his face, let it fly. Away it flew for the target, but alas, instead of striking in the center it struck out near the edge of the target, farther from the center than any other arrow. He had missed. He had done the poorest of any of the contestants.

Some of the spectators smiled covertly. Others laughed aloud at his poor shot. Some looked at him in surprise, for they had expected a good shot from him. But he had missed. He had failed of his purpose and now he stood before them chagrined, humiliated, ridiculed. How natural, under the circumstances, that he should feel discouraged! How natural that he should say within himself, "Well, I shall never try again. I shall never allow myself to be humiliated publicly again. If I cannot do better than that I will stop practicing archery altogether."

Would he be wise to do this? Should he not rather inquire why the arrow missed the mark? Why did he so fail in his purpose? Was he careless in his aim or in the manner of his shooting, or was there a flaw in his arrow? Perhaps the feathers on his arrow were not arranged properly, or possibly the bowstring slipped at one end. Perhaps a gust of wind caught the arrow and drove it out of its course. Was it his fault or was it a contingency against which he could not be prepared? Perhaps the miss was not his fault.

You and I, reader, may never have been archers and may never have observed such a contest, but we are engaged in life's contest. In our lives, we can look back, doubtless, upon many shots that missed. Many of our endeavors have brought us only failure. We have felt the humiliation of failure. We have felt the heart-burning that has come with the ridicule from others, the amused smile, the pitying look, or perhaps the contemptuous sneer. Oh, yes, you know how it feels to fail. You know how discouraging it is. Your hopes were high, your expectations kindled, your confidence assured, and then—you failed. The shot missed the target. You did not attain the expected result. Perhaps you tried to help someone. You said or did just what you thought would be the best, but you missed the mark. You saw and felt you had failed. You went away discouraged, and that discouragement stood in the way of your using your next opportunity or perhaps several opportunities to do something further. You realized you had done your best, but you had failed. You are keenly aware of it. The fact stands before you like a mountain.

Again you attempted to do something. Perhaps it was on an altogether different line. This time some weakness in yourself manifested itself just when you needed your strength most, and you failed. Your purpose was good, but you failed. More than likely you have had a thousand such experiences in your life. You realize you have failed in many things. Sometimes you have not been able to carry out your intentions. Sometimes unexpected circumstances have arisen to dash your plans to the earth. Sometimes other

people have consciously or unconsciously thrown
hindrances in your way. Sometimes your own
weaknesses or your faults or your carelessness,
your lack of forethought, your unwise methods,
or something else brought your hopes and purposes in a wreck at your feet.

There is always humiliation and discouragement in failure whether that failure results from
our own faults or from things quite beyond our
control or something we could not foresee. We
often fail because we do not know all the forces
that are working and cannot foresee the con-
tingencies that we must face. Sometimes we fail
and do not know why we fail. What shall we do
when we fail? Fold our arms and sit in idleness
with downcast head and discouraged hearts? Ah,
no, there is a better way. The old saying is, "If
at first you don't succeed, try, try again." Unless
we follow this motto in our life we shall inevitably fail to be all we ought to be and all we may
be. Life is usually made of success and failure. No
one can hope always to succeed. No one can
hope that all his efforts shall be fruitful. We know
too well the weakness and inefficiency of humanity to believe that we can always win.

Success depends upon so many things that we are likely to overlook some of them. The thing we overlook is very often so essential that there can be no success without it. Sometimes we fail because there are factors in the case of which we do not know. Not knowing them, we cannot provide against them. Sometimes we think we are stronger or wiser or more able than we are. Sometimes we fail when we feel we ought not to have failed. This is the kind of failure that stings us most. No matter what sort of failure we make nor how great that failure, there is one thing we ought never to do, but it is very natural to do this very thing. It is so natural that we will find ourselves doing it before we realize it. That thing is to condemn ourselves. Perhaps we have been to blame for our failure. Heaping condemnation upon ourselves is not going to help matters even in such a case. Meet the things as they are, but do not become your own persecutor.

Instead of being discouraged by our failures, we should summon our resolution. We should determine that we will not be balked, that our lives shall not be failures, then we shall conquer our weaknesses and our faults.

TWO PHASES OF RELIGION

LIFE is many-sided and has divers variations. This is true in any field of life, whether it be moral, social, business, or religious. It is sometimes supposed that in religious life everyone should have the same experience and should manifest it in the same way. There is no more reason for believing this should be true than that things in any other department of life should be brought down to a dead level. There is variety in religious experiences. No two persons have the same experience in all details, nor in their outlook upon religious matters nor in their attitude toward religious things.

It is true that all Christians have the same basis for their religion, namely, their faith in Christ and their acceptance of him through the remission of their sins and the new birth. But even in these things there is a variety of experiences, a variety of manifestations, and a variety of results. This variety is not objectionable, but the reverse. There are many phases of experience just as there are many phases of Christian belief, but there are two phases which we desire to notice at this time. They are the mystical phase and the practical phase. We see these two phases manifested in two of the great false religions of the world. Buddhism is a type of religion that well illustrates the mystical or contemplative type. The images of Buddha always express quietness and soul peace. Buddha is a dreamer. He is lost in contemplation. He is absorbed in his own reflections. He is an idealist. He is not disturbed by the stress and strife of life about him. He sits there calm, unmoved, alone in his thoughts. The whirl and hurry of life mean nothing to him.

What are the consequences of these characteristics upon the followers of Buddha? His scholarly followers love contemplation. This may enrich the soul and the mind. It may bring an inner peace which then comes as the result of mere detachment from the ordinary things of life. On the ordinary people the effect has been to produce a multitude of idle, lazy priests, who make their religion only an excuse for their indolence. Buddhism does not inspire effort; it does not result in progress; it does not produce forcefulness, but instead weakness. This we see illustrated in the nations which are followers of Buddha.

On the other hand, we have an illustration of the opposite phase of religion in Mohommedanism. It is a remarkable contrast to Buddhism. Mohammed was aggressive, determined, purposeful. He seized the sword and inspired his followers with warlike enthusiasm. His followers today are aggressive, determined, mighty in purpose. Their aggregate will to spread the faith and to oppose other faiths is very powerful. Mohammedanism is sweeping down through Africa, making greater conquests by far than Christianity in that continent. Two things occasion this. First, its lack of the lofty ideals and principles of Christianity, so that its appeal is to the baser passions, with the promise of their gratification in the world to come. Second, its aggressiveness, joined with its low moral requirements, pushes it forward faster than the high ideals of Christianity can be pushed forward. Nevertheless, it lacks those qualities that will render it permanent when it comes into conflict with the more powerful principles of Christianity.

But to return to the Christian religion. The opposite characteristics represented by Buddhism and Mohammedanism have their reflections in Christianity. There are those of the mythical type who love to dream. They are worshipful, devotional, idealistic; their enjoyment comes from contemplation. They delight in lofty thoughts and noble principles. We cannot get along without this type of Christianity, but this type of itself would never save the world. Its tendency is rather to withdraw itself into some monastery or to some lofty height. Buddha can sit in calm contemplation, peaceful and restful, with terrible evils all around him. There are Christians who can do the same. There must be the dreamers, but there must also be the practical realists who not only have religion in their heads and hearts but in their muscles also. There must be the men of vision, the seers. There must also be the workers.

Christianity must have the practical men of affairs. Dreams must be made realities. Christianity of the cloister must be balanced with active zeal. The early church won its way through the world not only because it had a high vision, but because it had a mind to work.

It had a message to proclaim and proclaimed it. Christianity in the heart bears fruit in the outer life. A heart full of divine love is dynamic. Activity is the moral expression of grace in the heart. Love is not content merely to gaze upon and contemplate the objects of its adoration. It must *do* something for that object. Love is a motive force. It must find some method of expression. Love is never satisfied to dwell in self while the world is being lost. The highest type of Christianity is that in which the two phases of religion are united. There must be the worshipful, the devotional, the thoughtful. There must be contemplation and consideration. There must be idealism. But these things must be united with zeal, activity, and work. There must be the practical application of the principles of Christianity. There must be work, and much of it, in order to build up the cause of Christ and to lead men into Christian living and into aggressive hostility to the evils that are all around us.

The dreamer who sits Buddha-like, with all the evils that surround him unnoticed, exerts little influence to make men better. He dwells afar from others. He is a negative rather than a positive force. On the other hand, the practical man who is full of zeal but who has not that background of idealism and thoughtfulness often fails. He needs the mystical in his life to give it the proper quality. He must have the devotional to bring grace into his practical work. Zeal and faith must be united. There is a great deal of what is supposed to be Christian work done that never amounts to anything. There is a great deal of zeal manifested that never produces any practical results. The reason is that there is not that inner content of divine love and grace to give it power. Just as contemplative Christianity without the ardor of a practical zeal is largely fruitless, so zeal and activity without genuine devotion and piety and a warm responsive love can never be effective. It may accomplish something, but its results will be meager and of poor quality. It may build up organization; it may create a great stir, but its results will not be enduring. Love cannot be content to love afar in restful contemplation. It must bestir itself. Zeal without love is a busybody without tools. To successful Christians and successful Christian workers, we must combine both phases of religion. We must take time for meditation and prayer, for contemplation and introspection. We must cultivate noble ideals and high aspirations. But we must not be content with this alone. We must also be practical. We must give expression to our ideals in zealous labors and in continuous activity. We must let the floods that are produced by contemplation and devotion burst forth to water the world. If we are practical and tend to neglect the spiritual and contemplative, we should correct this neglect by overcoming it and by developing the mystical in our nature. If we are so mystical that we are impracticable and accomplish little but dreaming, we should stir up our zeal into activity and be busy for the Lord.

Combining these two phases of Christianity, we shall certainly be successful in our labors for the Lord and in our Christian lives and experiences.

DOING THINGS LOVE'S WAY

NOT everything goes to please us in this world. Things displease us; people displease us; circumstances are not what we wish they were. There are many things to try and to vex us. How often we need forbearance, patience, self-control! How often the impulse comes, when things do not go to suit us, to speak hastily, to act uncharitably, or to behave ourselves in an uncomely way! When we are displeased, the mind resents it. The strength of this resentment depends upon the strength of our displeasure and upon the discipline we have used upon ourselves. It depends somewhat, also, upon the natural disposition, for even when the heart has been purified, the natural disposition remains.

People will not always do as we desire them to do or feel that they ought to do. They will not even do as they know they ought to do. Some people will misuse us or even abuse us. Untruths and misrepresentations there will be, going from mouth to mouth, about us. We shall be criticized.

We cannot always have our own way. Seeing this is sure to be true, we must adjust ourselves to conditions and meet circumstances in a way that is consistent with real Christian character. We shall have difficulties to meet in the home, in business, in the church, in fact, in every relation of life that brings us into contact with other human beings. Their actions, desires, attitudes, and such like will inevitably limit and restrict us in some way. These restrictions are likely to chafe us. We are likely to resent them. And too, we are so constituted that we naturally desire things to go as we wish them to and as we think they ought to go. We naturally think our way is best. Since it is human nature to feel this way about things and since if we follow out the natural trend of such feeling we shall act selfishly and without due regard for others, it becomes necessary for us to mark out a way for ourselves and deliberately walk in that way. We must set a standard of conduct for ourselves and deliberately live up to that standard, regardless of feelings, circumstances, or conditions about us.

True charity is love. God is love, and we are told in essence that if we are God's, if we are his true children indeed, his love is shed abroad in our hearts by the Holy Spirit. If this love is shed abroad in our hearts it will warm all the cold emotions. It will soften all the asperities of our natures. It will quicken every noble impulse. It will give us a sympathetic generosity. It will write the law of kindness in our hearts. There is no limit to the blessed working of divine love in the human soul, when that soul is fully surrendered to Him. But divine love in the heart is not necessarily a continuous thing. We may lose that love out of our hearts. Even when it is in our hearts it does not do away with those natural things, those tendencies and dispositions that are in us. It has a strong influence upon them, but they are still there. They must be guarded. They are needful to us. Without them we should not be complete, but with them, we must be on our guard.

We must not let impulse rule our lives. We must do what we *ought* to do, not what we feel disposed to do. Usually we know what we ought to do and could do it if we would, but often, in order to do it, we must take hold upon ourselves and sometimes even put a severe restraint upon some of our impulses and feelings. If we are to dwell in love, which is to dwell in God, we must let love work out through us. We must give it free course in our lives. We must give it full freedom to work. We must compel those things within us that would hinder the operation of love, in its normal way, to give place to its work.

The will must control these elements and say to love, "I will restrain these hindering things that thou mayest work as thou wilt." But how many times these things within us are allowed to work, hampering, hindering, and preventing love's operation. It is within our power to give place to whichever we will. We can put love in the background and act according to impulse and natural desire or inclination, or we can master these and give love freedom to work. Both elements cannot have full liberty. Imperious self would have its way. It must be made to bow to love and love must be given the right of way in the heart.

But what does it mean to do things in love's way? We have only to look at the things love does to know this. Love is never harsh. Love will restrain the tongue from many a bitter word. It will put kindness into the soul and kindness into the words. Love may be firm. It will be firm when it is necessary, but with all its firm-

ness, it will not be harsh. Harsh words on the
tongue mean that we give way to harsh feelings
in the heart. When there is harshness in the heart,
it shows itself in the words, attitude, and general
behavior toward others. It is because harshness
is given place in the heart that there are so many
"family jars" and so many church troubles.

Love is not self-willed. It rejoices in the prosperity and advancement of others. It is willing
to sacrifice its own way. It is willing to com-
promise the situation and make peace, even at
a loss to itself. Love is the cure for all family,
neighborhood, and church troubles, as well as
all national and international troubles. Love to
God means love to man. Love makes always for
peace, quietness, and contentment. Selfishness
is the basis of many church troubles. People want
their own way. They want to "boss" things. Or
if it does not manifest itself in that way, it does
in another way which shows the same principle;
that is, it refuses to submit. Love is willing to
submit when no principle is at stake. What is
the trouble then, when members of a congrega-
tion cannot submit to the rule of God through
their pastor? It is the lack of love. What is the
trouble when they cannot submit to each other?

A lack of love. What is the trouble when they have disagreements, hard feelings, loss of confidence? A lack of love.

Let us do things love's way. Let us ask ourselves the question, "What would love do?" "What would I do if I acted as love would act?" What attitude would I hold toward others?" "What disposition would I manifest toward them?" Let us, therefore, seek that love from God that is kind, gentle, easy to be entreated, full of mercy and good works, and let us manifest it to all about us. It will make others happy and will react in happiness in our own lives. If we do not have this abounding love in our souls, let us seek God until he gives it to us. Let us beware, on the other hand, that we do not allow the natural tendencies within us to forbid love to work its own way when love is within the heart.

THE GENESIS OF PEACE

THIS world is full of unrest and turmoil. There is turmoil in hearts and homes, in communities, churches, and nations, and there is international turmoil, until the world is a seething mass of unrest. People are longing for peace, but peace can begin only when the turmoil in the world is removed, and it is removed only by the eradication of its cause. Unrest, wherever found, indicates irritation. Unrest is a fever. It is a symptom that something is not going right somewhere.

When there is not peace in the heart it is because two forces are striving against each other. When the forces of nature are at rest everything is quiet and peaceful. But when the strong wind rages across the face of the sea, the wild waves toss and roar. When it wrestles with the mighty forces they sway and creak and strain. So it is in the human heart, in the family, the community, the church, the nation, and between the nations. Where there is not peace it is because there is irritation, and the only way to bring peace is to remove the source of irritation.

If we do not have peace with God it is because there is something causing irritation in the heart. One thing that causes irritation and destroys peace is sin. We never can have peace with God with sin in the heart. The soul can never be at rest with that quiet peaceable rest that comes from righteousness while indulging in sin of any sort or while sin that has been indulged in is unrepented of. But there is a remedy for sin. That remedy is available today. So, reader, if your heart is not at peace with God because of sin you may get that source of irritation out of your heart by confessing it and taking God's way out. Do this at once; then his peace will fill your soul.

Another source of irritation in the soul is unbelief. It is destructive of peace; so if we will have peace with God, calmness and rest in our souls, we may find it if we will believe in God. There is a sweet rest of soul that comes from trusting, a peace that may be known in no other way than by trusting. The doubts and fears that irritate and trouble, that destroy the peace and bring heaviness, discouragement, and sometimes almost despair, will vanish when belief comes into the heart and peace like the calm after a great storm will settle down over the soul. But peace cannot come so long as unbelief irritates and annoys the soul.

Another thing that prevents peace in many a soul is self-will. There is a lack of submission to God's will, and so the relation with God cannot be a relation of peace and sweet confident trust. To have peace we must rid ourselves of self-will. We must submit ourselves to the will of God. We must say from the bottom of our heart, "Not my will, but thine, be done." We must be willing actively to engage in doing his will. Then the peace of God which passeth all understanding will keep our hearts and minds and we shall know the blessedness of true rest of soul. Self-will is the cause of the lack of peace that exists in many families. This one feels he must have his way; that one feels she must have her way; and so there is a clashing of wills that brings irritation, unrest, dissatisfaction, and results in ill feeling, resentment, and bitterness. Self-will brings unhappiness wherever it operates. Self-will is selfish; it is inconsiderate of others; it asserts its own right to the exclusion of the rights of others. It will have its way, but when it has its way it brings sorrow and unrest. Peace flies away from self-will. It cannot abide in the same heart or in the same home with this destroyer of happiness.

Self-will in the church is the cause of more trouble than any other one thing. That disposition to demand that things go the way we think they ought to go and the setting up of our will above the will of others, the winning of our way, may give us temporary pleasure of a certain sort. It may give us a selfish satisfaction that comes from having our own way, but it will destroy the peace of the church and the peace of our own hearts. Submitting our will is the hardest thing we have to do, but it is the thing we must do before we can have true peace. Self-will is based on pride. Where there is contention in the family, in the community, in the church, in the nation, we can easily locate the trouble. We can easily find the root of the matter. The wise man tells us that "only by pride cometh contention" (Prov. 13:10). Here the destroyer of peace is traced back to his den. Excess of self-esteem, which is a form of pride, causes people to be self-willed, and self-will destroys peace.

The nations could be at peace if they would justly esteem each other and each other's rights, but this they will not do. In the same manner communities could be at peace, but pride bringeth contention. Homes could be at peace, churches could be at peace, if they would get rid of that pride that brings contention. It is useless to deny the source of contention. People do not feel disposed to contend unless they have pride in their hearts. To be sure we must contend for the faith sometimes, but this is quite another thing. We may contend for the faith in a thoroughly peaceable manner, or we may do so in a self-willed contentious manner. The latter never brings peace, but only turmoil and division.

Would you have peace with God? Do you wish rest, comfort, and happiness in your soul? God is not your enemy. His thoughts toward you are thoughts of peaceableness (Jer. 29:11), and he tells us that the effect of righteousness shall be peace (Isa. 32:17); so all we have to do to be at peace with God is to get rid of those disturbing elements in our own hearts and minds, get rid of our sins by trusting in Christ for salvation, get rid of all unbelief by taking God at his word and trusting him sincerely, get rid of our self-

will through the blood of Christ and through
submitting our wills to God—then we may have
peace with God and peace within ourselves. We
shall have "all joy and peace in believing" (Rom.
15:13). But to keep this peace we must follow
after the things that make for peace (Rom.
14:19). We must "seek peace, and pursue it."
We must do those things that belong to peace.
We must hold that attitude that brings peace. We
must be just to ourselves and believe in ourselves to have peace; not condemning ourselves,
but being fair to ourselves. Peace will begin and
peace will abide when those things are removed
which destroy peace.

THE SWEETEST JUICE

THERE is an oriental proverb which says, "The first juice that flows from the grapes is always the sweetest; crushed grapes are sure to give out the flavor of the skin." Recently my eyes fell upon this proverb and it set me to thinking. How many sermons nature preaches to us! How many things in the spiritual world have their counterpart in natural things! When I thought of the sweet, luscious grapes cast into the wine press, bursting of their own weight and the sweet juice running out without the application of external pressure, I thought of the difference between two kinds of service.

I thought how many Christians are urged on to service by a feeling of duty. I remembered how many times in my own life I had felt that I *ought* to do something or that I *must* do something and had acted from that consideration. To be sure there is a blessing in even that kind of service. There is the sense of having done one's duty. There is the sense of having filled God's requirement. There is a sense of being blameless in the matter. But ah, how much richer and sweeter and fuller the service that is the outpouring of love, the service that flows out of itself from a heart bursting with love—that pent-up love which, when it reaches out and finds an avenue of service, delights in that service! How the heart is enriched by doing such service! How love rejoices at the opportunity! How the joy-bells are set ringing!

On the other hand, the service that is "squeezed out" is like the wine when the powerful pressure is applied to the grapes. There is a different flavor in the wine; there is a different flavor in the service, and that different flavor detracts from the quality, both of the wine and of the service. Service that is based on duty is always in a measure compulsory, but service that is the out-flowing of love runs ahead of duty and is always free. It feels no compulsion, but the compulsion of desire. It is its meat to do the will of the Father, its delight to anticipate his will. It seeks opportunity to expend itself. It does not have to be coaxed nor constrained. There is no reluctance in it.

Paul laid down a basis for acceptable service saying, "Every man according as he purposeth in his heart, so let him give; not grudgingly, or of necessity: for God loveth a cheerful giver. And God is able to make all grace abound toward you; that ye, always having all sufficiency in all things, may abound to every good work" (II Cor. 9:7-8). Here we find three elements that enter into service, or three kinds of service. Paul is applying it especially to giving, but the principles apply to every kind of service. We are to give as we purpose in our hearts, but this purposing may be in three different ways. It may be grudgingly, that is reluctantly, with a feeling that we should be glad if we did not have to do it; that we should be glad if God did not ask it, or that we should be glad if there were no necessity of its being done. Such a disposition of mind would prefer that there were no need for service, but since there is to be service, it will give, but it would prefer to withhold.

There are so many who serve in this way. There are things that must be done for the cause. There is need of accomplishment, but the lips, and if not the lips perhaps the heart, says, "Oh, dear, I wish it did not have to be done"; or, "I wish someone else would do it." However, even then they may purpose to do it since it has to be done, but there is little joy or sweetness in such service.

Again, there is the service of necessity—a feeling that if I do not do certain things God will condemn me and my conscience will condemn me, or my brethren or my neighbors will condemn me; and so, to retain God's favor and the approval of my conscience and the confidence of my fellow men, I feel under the necessity of giving or serving, and thus I serve. How many people there are who do things because they feel they cannot be easy in their conscience if they do not! Well, they have their reward, even for such service. It is the reward of an approving conscience. But how little either of these two forms of service is acceptable, either to God or to ourselves! We have within ourselves a consciousness that such a service is not the kind of service that can be freely given or freely received. It is better than no service, but how much better service than this we are capable of giving!

The third sort of service which men purpose to give is expressed thus, "God loveth a cheerful giver." It is the unforced giving, the uncompelled service, that enriches both the server and the one served. Cheerful, ready, willing service brings immediate reward, but such service is never done with a view to receiving the reward, for the service is counted higher than the reward. But there is something that lies back of willing service. This is set forth in the eighth verse: "God is able to make all grace abound toward you; that ye, always having all sufficiency in all things, may abound to every good work." Willing service has a background of grace, and that is just the reason willing service is always an easy service. The task may be difficult; it may require the exertion of all our powers and determined perseverance; but if there be a willing mind the service is easy, because the ease of the service lies in the willingness with which we undertake the task. Ofttimes service is hard because there is lack of grace, and grace is lacking because willingness is lacking; but if there first be a ready mind to serve, then grace makes service easy. God is able to make all grace abound toward us, and he will do so if there be the ready mind and the open heart to receive it; but the reluctant mind is a barrier to grace, that leaves the heart void, and whatever service may be rendered is a compulsory service, a wine that has in it the taste of the skins of the grapes.

What is the voice that speaks in our heart today? What does it say to us? The sense of duty says, "I must." Grace and love say, "I may." In the one case is the urgent necessity, in the other the glad joy of love because its desire is gratified. Which voice is in your heart? Which prompts you to action? Is it I must or I may?

THE EASIEST WAY

A FARMER was passing through his field one day when he observed a hole in the fence. As he was weary from his labors, instead of properly repairing the fence he stuck a piece of a rail in the hole and went his way. The next morning he found half a dozen hogs in his cornfield and spent an hour or so getting them out and making proper repairs on the fence. Considerable destruction had also been done in the field to the growing crop. He had taken the easiest way, as it seemed, but in the end it proved to be the hardest way.

A timberman broke his log chain. Instead of having it properly repaired he took the easiest way, as it seemed to him, and fastened the chain together with wire. A few days later he was some miles from home loading logs when the repaired place in the chain broke. This time he had no wire, so he was compelled to unhitch his team and go several miles to the repair shop and lost nearly a half day of valuable time.

Doing things the easiest way often proves to be doing them the poorest way, the costliest way, and in the end the hardest way, but the farmer who does this may be known by the looks of his barnyard and buildings. The merchant who does this comes to bankruptcy. The mechanic who does this loses his job. In the spiritual life, though, many follow these examples even when they know the outcome cannot be good. They see some duty they ought to do, but they let it go undone. They see some progress they ought to make that would require an effort on their part, but they just let go and risk all, hoping that someway, somehow it will come out all right anyway. How easy it is to say, "Oh, just let it go!" This is the easiest way for the time being, but in the end is it really the easiest way? Are not such people constantly reproached by their conscience for their neglect? Do they not miss the joy and peace and satisfaction of heart that come from the knowledge of duty well done? Is not the loss of an approving conscience in these matters greater than the effort it would take to do duty and to do it properly?

Neglect in the present, just letting things drift, makes the future harder. It robs one of a thousand blessings. It often fills the soul with regret and sometimes with remorse. So the easiest way cannot be neglect of duty. Neglect of opportunities, neglect to measure up to God's expectations or the expectations of our brethren, while it may be easy for the moment is harder in the end and often becomes disastrous. So when in spiritual things you are tempted to say, "Just let it go," whether you say it to another or say it to your own soul, means you are choosing the hardest way in at least nine cases out of ten. The present ease will mean future hardness, and usually dissatisfaction and regret. The easiest way of all is to do what ought to be done when it ought to be done, and in the way it ought to be done. Then the conscience and the mind are at rest and we feel a gratifying sense of satisfaction in duty well done.

When we do attempt a thing, whether it be some labor, some duty toward others, self-cultivation, or whatever it may be, we are many times tempted to choose the method that requires the least labor without regard to the final results. We feel we must do *something*, but perhaps there is not a willingness to exert oneself to the extent necessary to do the thing the best way. The artisan who does this soon has the reputation of being a poor workman. The farmer who does this raises poor crops. The preacher who does this preaches poor sermons. The Christian who does this is not a progressive and thoroughly happy and blessed Christian. What is really easiest in the end is that which is best. When we use the best method we get the best results. When we slight our work we always pay dearly for our attempt to do things the easiest way.

When one of those neglectful Christians who does things the way that seems the easiest for the moment gets sick or gets into serious difficulty or under a heavy trial, he pays very dearly for his indolent attitude hitherto. He is where he needs grace and strength, where he needs to be vigorous and strong, where he needs a good conscience and a confident assurance. He does not have these. Therefore, his battle will be much harder to win, his difficulties will be harder to overcome. He wonders why his trials are heavier than those of others. The trouble is he has weakened himself by taking the easiest way. He has neglected to strengthen the weak places. He has omitted doing what he knew he ought to do, and now he must pay the full penalty for it.

His past ease must now be made good by great labors. When we slight the present we rob the future. When we rob the future we incur a debt we must surely pay in that future day. Many have repaid such debts with tears and heart-aches, with sorrows and struggles, with defeats and sometimes with disasters. How much easier it is in the end when we have done things properly all the way along!

Sometimes people think the easiest way is the way that requires the least sacrifice. They know it would be better if they should sacrifice something to gain the end desired, but they refuse to sacrifice, and take the easier way. They miss the reward of sacrifice. They miss the satisfaction of work well done and often regret not having made the sacrifice. Sometimes to do things as they ought to be done requires humiliation, self-abasement, and the condition of being misunderstood by others. Those who are not willing to humble themselves often seek for an easier way, a way which will not humiliate them, but what they do can never satisfy their own souls. Whenever they think of the matter there will be an inward unrest. There will be a sense of having come short of God's real purpose and of having missed an opportunity of which they should have taken the fullest advantage. They have really done the thing in the hardest way, and the humiliation they shunned led to an inward humiliation that will last longer even though it was not greater at the time.

Let us do things as we ought to do them. Let us live as we ought to live, sacrifice as we ought to sacrifice, and measure up to the full standard of the truth. Then we shall have the satisfaction of duty well done. We shall have the approval of our conscience. We shall have the approval of God. We shall have that peace that passeth all understanding. We shall have grace to meet our trials, temptations, and difficulties. We shall be strong in the Lord and in the power of his might. But if we do things the easiest way we shall be weak and faltering, we shall have a thousand difficulties we should not otherwise have, and we can never develop that rich fullness of Christian experience that we are privileged to have if we will do things as they ought to be done.

OUR BLESSED HOPE

YESTERDAY a funeral passed our home. The solemn procession moved slowly onward toward the cemetery gate a few squares away. The muffled sounds of the passing cars of a funeral cortege as they pass my window always tell a melancholy tale. A beloved voice is silent forever to earth. A heart has ceased to beat. A life has reached its end. Solemnly the words "Dust to dust, and ashes to ashes" are spoken. The mourning friends go their way. Only a newly made mound in the cemetery remains to tell the story.

What, is this all? Is dust to dust and ashes to ashes the final end of the being who was once vibrant with life and joyous with vigorous energy? To every soul there comes the age-old inquiry, "If a man die, shall he live again?"

Time summons all, both rich and poor, both high and low, both great and small, to stand before the open grave and to answer in their inmost souls this old query. Let us follow the quiet procession, and let us inquire of each comer what

is his hope for the future? Here comes a modern
Sadducee. He is a materialist. He believes not in
angel or spirit. Man to him is only brother of
the beast. Death ends all. As one such said to me,
"A man is just like a horse; when he dies, that is
the end." The open grave closes above the form
beloved to him and leaves him bereaved of hope.
To him life is a past that comes to its end upon
a great cliff, beyond which there is nothing but
space. To him the grave is a melancholy place.
It is the end of all his plans and dreams, of all his
hopes and expectations. When those whom he
loves go from him at the call of death, it leaves
only a measureless void which nothing can ever
fill, and which he never expects to be filled.

Behind the materialist comes the atheist, with
eyes downcast. To him there is no God, no power
which can say to death, "Stand back." For him
there is no voice of consolation or of comfort.
Hope is dead; her voice is no longer heard.

Next in order comes the deist. He believes in
God, but the God in whom he believes is a far-
away, unknown being who has no part in the
life or death of man, who has no interest in what
concerns him, a God who has gone off and for-
gotten. The deist pauses beside the newly made

grave. This to him is the end of all. He also is without hope beyond it.

After him an agnostic draws near. He does not know; he cannot find out. Perhaps life has not come to its final conclusion; he does not know. There may be something beyond the grave; he cannot tell. He knows nothing for certain. He is in doubt about everything. He knows no way to resolve his doubts. And so he stands before the newly made grave, and the wreath that he places upon it is an interrogation point.

Next comes the infidel. Perhaps there is a sneering smile upon his face. Frankly, he does not believe. He knows the Bible says there will be a resurrection, but the Bible is not God's book, in his judgment. So he believes only what it pleases him to believe of the present or the future. Perhaps he believes in immortality, but what does he believe of it, and upon what grounds does he believe it? If he believes in the resurrection, he does not know why he believes it. His hope has no true basis. He rejects the only basis that is given him, and so if he will but admit it, he must, like the agnostic, only question.

Next comes the philosopher. His philosophy may show him there is a life beyond the grave.

It may say to him that since the race believes in immortality, since they have an inner consciousness of immortality, and since so many things in nature seem to argue from analogy that there shall be a resurrection, he may conclude there is a resurrection, that there is a life beyond the grave. But what that life is like, or whether it is a certainty, he cannot tell. His philosophy falters. It is insufficient. And he, like those before him, is left to question.

Next comes the scientist. His science has not found the human soul. He does not know it as an entity. He cannot weigh it or measure it. The laws of chemistry do not reveal it. He finds strange things in man which he cannot explain. But they do not tell him of immortality. He does not know from his science whether there is anything beyond the grave.

Behind him comes the worldling, who finds his all in self, or riches, or fame. He lives for this world alone. He has not stopped to inquire about eternity. He has been quite content to occupy himself with the things of the present life. He has scarcely thought about anything beyond the grave. Indeed, he will not let the thought of the grave come into his mind when he can help it.

Perhaps he believes in immortality in a casual way, but it seems nothing to him. It is unreal, uncertain; and if he has a dim, vague hope, it is a hope based on nothing trustworthy, nothing that can be the real basis of a hope. And he, like those before him, is one of those whom the Bible pictured as "having no hope."

Look again at this company and you will see them all silent before the newly made grave. No voice comforts them; they have no words to comfort another. Death is a leap into the dark. Beyond is only the great unknown.

Only the Christian has hope in his death. His hope in death is not a hope in himself. His hope is in a person, the Lord Jesus Christ—he who was dead, but is alive forevermore. He believes in him who said, "I am the resurrection, and the life: he that believeth in me, though he were dead, yet shall he live." And this hope is called our "blessed hope"; it is the one great hope of the Christian. As we have this hope, death has no terrors for us, and we can say, "O death, where is thy sting? O grave, where is thy victory?" And so it comes that believing this so many Christians go down into the valley of the shadow with a smile of joy upon their countenances and with an unwavering faith in their hearts. Only the eye of faith sees beyond the grave. Only the tongue that speaks through faith hath words to break the silence with the clear joy tones of triumph. Faith stands before the newly made grave and falters not. And the Christian, though sorrowful, is always rejoicing, for with the eye of faith he sees beyond the present into the glorious eternity, and his heart doubts not.

There are three phases of our hope, or three things to which hope looks forward in expectancy. The first is the coming of Jesus our Lord (Titus 2:13). We have hope in him, not merely for the present life but for the life which is to come (I Cor. 15:19; Acts 24:15). Through him we look forward to being "children of the resurrection," hoping and believing that it shall be according to his word that we shall nevermore die and that we shall be equal to the angels, that we shall possess everlasting life through the eternal ages and dwell at the right hand of God.

This hope of eternal life is not a new thing. It is older than the world. Paul speaks of the "hope of eternal life, which God, that cannot lie, promised before the world began" (Titus 1:2). God planned eternal life for us. He promised it to us before we had an existence. And so we look forward with eager expectancy that sinks not into the grave, but goes beyond it and rejoices in the eternal ages of God. This is the blessed hope, the anchor of the Christian soul.

STEALING THE SUNSHINE

IT IS related that it was the custom of the teacher of a certain kindergarten to have one of her pupils mark on the blackboard each day to represent the weather. She had colored crayons, and different colors represented the different kinds of weather: white for snow, gray for cloudy, yellow for sunshine, etc. A child was permitted, as a reward of good conduct, to go each day and make the drawing on the board to represent that day's weather. One day a little boy was permitted to go to the board for this purpose. In looking in the crayon box, he failed to find the yellow crayon, which represented the sunshine. After looking vainly, he cried out, "Somebody has stolen the sunshine."

Somebody had taken away that which represented the sunshine. And so there are "somebodys," and all too many of them in the world, who take away the sunshine from someone's life. Many lives are dark and sad, not because of what the persons themselves do, but because of what

others do. It is true we often shut out our own
sunshine. Our own conduct often plunges us
into darkness, sorrow, and grief, if we do not
follow God's will. But there are many who do
right themselves and who might have sunshine
if others would give them an opportunity. How
many families are unhappy where they might
be happy! How many husbands and wives make
their companions unhappy, and often very mis-
erable when there is no need of it! How many
parents darken the lives of their children! How
many children bring sorrow and suffering to
their parents! How often brethren and sisters in
the church cast a shadow over someone's life!
They become sunshine thieves. They steal someone's sunshine, and worst of all they are no better for it themselves, but worse. If a man steals
because he is hungry or has not sufficient cloth-
ing, we can more easily excuse him than we can
the one who steals when he has no such need.
So the one who takes the sunshine from any life
by any act that is not necessary or that serves
no good purpose is entirely inexcusable. Not a
thing can be said in approval of his conduct.

One way of stealing people's sunshine is to
criticize them. When a person feels that he has

done his best he naturally feels that what he has done merits approval. But if, instead of this he receives criticism, if someone makes light of his work or sneers at what he has done, he feels discouraged. He feels like not trying again. All the pleasure he had in his work has gone. The critic has stolen his sunshine, and the critic is not helped thereby. It is true some things must be criticized. Some people's conduct must be criticized. But there is always a way to do this that will be encouraging instead of discouraging. If we must criticize someone's work, let us do it in a helpful way. Let us first point out the good qualities in it. Let us say what we can in praise of it. Let us give our approval as far as approval can be given. Then let us suggest that it might have been done better another way; or, "You can improve on this particular part thus." Or, "Do you not thing it would be better to do this part of it thus?" or, "Did you ever try doing it this way?" This is constructive criticism. This is criticism that does not discourage. This is being helpful rather than hindering. So if you must criticize people, be sure not to take their sunshine from them in doing it. Approval encourages. Condemnation discourages.

Another way that sunshine is stolen from people is by whispering forebodings. Some people are always looking forward to the future with the expectation that something bad will happen. There will be trouble; there will be sickness; something is going to happen; what gloomy prophecies they make. They are always throwing cold water on everything. They are always saying, "Look out now, you have to watch people." Oh, yes, reader, you know people of this sort. They are always croaking like a raven; they are always prophets of evil. The atmosphere about them is always discouraging. No matter how bright the prospect before them or anyone else, they are always ready to say: "Oh, yes, but just wait, something will happen." This, that, or the other will spoil things, and they are ready with their gloomy prophecies at any moment. Some of these people are glad to do something to make their prophecies come true. They take pleasure in making things more difficult for others.

We cannot afford to take any of the brightness or joy out of the life of anyone—not even a little child. Let us increase the sunshine instead of diminishing it. Let us add to the sum of joy in the world. Let us lift up, and not cast down.

THE ESSENCE OF CHRISTIAN LIVING

COAL tar is a dark, sticky, unattractive substance of little apparent value. But by chemical processes a great number of different chemicals are extracted from it which are used for many purposes. Some make dyes, some flavors, and by properly combining others rich perfumes of various sorts are produced. Looking at the dark, unlovely coal tar, we should not dream that it contained anything so desirable, but under the magic of the chemist's power many things are brought out of it to serve useful purposes.

The human heart in its natural state is unlovely. It is like the coal tar. But when the divine Chemist by his wisdom and power separates the evil from the good and makes Christians out of sinners, he produces a life-power within, so that we may live a life within and without that will have the same purpose and beauty as the lives of the angels in paradise. But Christian living is not a single thing. It is a compound. It is made up of a number of things. Four of these we shall notice

116

The first element that goes to make up Christian living of the attractive and worth-while kind is living *near* to Christ. The Bible teaches that the Christian lives in a close relation with Christ. We are "no more foreigners and strangers," but children of the Most High. We are no more "afar off," but are "brought nigh by the blood of Christ." His invitation is, "Come unto me." So to live the kind of Christian life that will breathe out a fragrance to all those about us we must live *near* to Christ. It is our privilege to live near to him. There are too many who live too far away from him. To them he is "Lord and Master." He is enthroned in majesty, and seems all too unapproachable.

This is the Christ of the universe. This is our Christ. But it is only one side of his character; still it is the only side that some people seem to see. He is not alone Lord and Master. He is Brother; he is Savior; he is Keeper; he is Companion along the way. He dwells in our hearts. It is not his relation of Lord and Master which brings out in us the beauty of Christian character, but that more intimate relation of Brother and Friend. It is the Christ to whom we draw near in full assurance of faith without fear, and without shrinking, without timidity, and without a sense of his overpowering greatness.

Christ is our Lord and Master, but he condescends also to come down upon a level with us and lets us approach him in the same familiar way as Mary approached him when she sat at his feet, and as the disciples did in their daily intercourse, and as the children did in their play. Ah, yes, we can draw near him unafraid, unabashed by his greatness, or by the sense of our weakness. We can live near him every day. We can be in the inner circle of his friends. We can have his presence with us. We can have with him that sweet sense of understanding that we have with our dearest and most-loved friends. Yea, he comes closer than even our dearest friends. He understands where they cannot understand. He can help where they cannot help.

So we need to come close to Christ, to live close to him. We need to cultivate that intimate relation, that union of soul which gives one a continued sense of his presence and friendship, and more than all, of his tender love. Without this intimate, personal sense of Christ's being with us and helping us, understanding us, and shedding the beneficent influence of his life over us, our life will lack one of the sweetest qualities of genuine Christianity. It is our blessed privilege to be near him. But to have this association we must cultivate a nearness to him and a sense of nearness to him by daily drawing near to him, and communing with him and pouring out our love to him. There is nothing that draws us to Christ like loving him. And love is cultivated by drawing near to him each day and many times a day, and pouring out our soul's love and devotion to him. We can live near him even in the most troublous times. And when we live near him our lives will never be stale nor lack the sweet perfume of holiness.

A second element of Christian living is that we shall live *by* Christ. So many when they are asked if they are Christians say, "I am trying to do the best I can. I am trying to live right." But they realize their trying is in their own human strength. Try as we will in this way, we can only fail, for we are to live Christians *by* Christ. We are to draw from him the strength and grace which will supplement what things we have and will equip us to meet the difficulties of life and to overcome them. But it is only by drawing from Christ day by day the things that are needful, the counsel, the wisdom, the understanding, and such like, that we can live as we know we ought to live. But the grace of Christ is free, and we have but to come to him, draw upon that grace, and use it together with what strength we have, and we shall be, not simply trying, but accomplishing; not straining and struggling, but living natural and victorious lives.

It is only when we realize our own inability to live up to the Christian standard by our own efforts and strength that we feel the need of other help. How much we are conscious of this! But all too many who are thus conscious of their need fail to get their daily need supplied, because they do not take those steps that are necessary to draw from Christ the needed help. We must live by Christ. There must be the daily inflowing of divine grace. We must feel as did Paul, that we trust not in ourselves, but in the living God. Then we must go forward, drawing from Christ each day by seeking his help, by opening our hearts that they may be filled, by communion with him, by earnest seeking. Christ is our life, and by him we must live if we live at all as he would have us live. But there is no holding back on his part. He gives freely to those who ask him. He satisfieth the longing soul. But many are too occupied by other things to seek that daily portion of Christ that they must have to live successfully. For them life cannot have the richness and the usefulness that might be theirs for the seeking.

Another of the essentials of Christian living is that we live *for* Christ. To the extent that we are occupied with self and with self-interests, to that extent we narrow the limits of Christian life. Life must be lived for Christ to be Christian life. It must be dedicated life. The language of our soul must be, "I'll live for him who died for me." The life of unselfish devotion to the interests of Christ is the life that shines with beauty and that has a sweet perfume. "Ye are not your own," says the apostle. The more we cast out selfishness, the less we seek our own, the more we yield ourselves to Christ and his work, the more we live with the purpose of pleasing him—the deeper and richer will be the current of the joy of living and of his grace that flows through our soul. If our Christian life is not satisfactory let us look into our hearts and see whether we are living for Christ or for self. To the extent we are living for self, to that extent we are robbing ourselves and robbing God. We are robbing ourselves of that blessedness that comes from wholehearted devotion to his interests. We are robbing God of the service that we ought to give him and of the opportunities to work through us as he would. And this is the very secret of the dearth and emptiness in the lives of many professors of Christianity. They are living for self, not for Christ; and the happiness that comes from selfishness is the lowest of all forms of happiness.

When we live near Christ and by Christ and for Christ there will be a fourth element seen in our lives. We shall live *like* Christ. The characteristics that were seen in him will be seen in us. We shall bear the fruits of the Spirit. We shall not show hatred, bitterness, envy, malice, nor any of the thousand other evils that spring from the natural heart. We shall be able to live like him; then we can say, "For me to live is Christ," and with joy we can add, "To die is gain."

So let us join in our lives these four elements of Christian living and we shall bear all the fruits of righteousness—and peace, joy, happiness, and contentment will be ours; and we shall lead natural, useful, and blessed Christian lives and inspire others to give their hearts to Christ.

"MY DADDY WON'T LET YOU"

A LITTLE boy was walking along a road one day when he met two larger boys. They sought to have some fun with the little fellow by teasing him. One began to threaten the little fellow to frighten him. That he was startled and that a pang of fear went through him was evident, but in a moment the little fellow had mastered himself. He braced up, looked his tormentor in the face, and in reply to the threat that had been made said positively, "No you won't." "Yes I will," said the other menacingly. "No you won't," said the little fellow. "My daddy won't let you."

Ah, there was the secret of his courage! His father was not in sight. Perhaps the child did not know where he was. However, he was confident of one thing—that his father would protect him and take care of him and let no ill befall him. This childlike confidence gave him courage to face the danger that seemed very real to him and to meet it without shrinking. What a lesson there is in this for us! This little fellow knew the situation was altogether too difficult for him. Either one of the two opponents was vastly superior to him in strength and could easily follow out any desire. Still his courage did not falter. He made no effort to run away. He faced the situation with confidence.

"My daddy won't let you." What a world of confident trust was wrapped up in these words! You and I, dear reader, have a Father who is as loving, as tender, as powerful—a millionfold, yea, infinitely greater in every respect than the father of this boy. If we, with the same simplicity of heart, meet the threatening situations upon our pathway and say to Satan and all his hosts, "My Father won't let you," with the same calm, abiding trust that the little boy showed, what strength it will give us, what courage for life's battles! Is there not just as much, yea, far more reason for us to be confident than the child had for his confidence? Our God is present; he is not out of sight nor hearing.

Our God is all powerful and he loves us with a love that never grows cold; that is, he is never indifferent to our welfare. There is ample ground for our confidence in God's multitude of promises,

every one of which is as safe to trust as his most
sacred oath. "Our Father will not let you," said
the three Hebrew children, and they walked un-
scathed through the fiery furnace. "My Father
won't let you," was Daniel's confidence in the
face of the roaring lions. The same words in different form were in the hearts of Isaiah and
Hezekiah when Jerusalem was surrounded by
the armies of Assyria. The leader of the enemies
of Judah told them they trusted in their God in
vain. See II Kings 18—19. He told them their God
could do no more than could the gods of the nations round about them, and that they had not
been able to save their countries from the ravag-
ing hosts of Assyria. But these embattled hosts
marched away and left Jerusalem untouched.
"Oh, it just happened that way. It was just a combination of circumstances," says the unbeliever.
Yes, it was a combination of circumstances, but
who combined the circumstances? Isaiah knew;
Hezekiah knew; the men of Jerusalem knew.

Nearly eight hundred years later Jerusalem
was again surrounded. This time it was the
Roman army. This time God did not say "Stay
within the walls," but "Flee." The Romans were
bent an destroying all the Jews within the city,

or sending them into captivity, but the Christians, forewarned of what was coming and being instructed what to do, looked upon the Roman armies without fear. They knew Jerusalem was to be destroyed. They knew that doubtless famine, pestilence, and great bloodshed were to follow. Many things threatened them from every side, but with a confidence born of trust in God they raised their eyes to heaven and said, "My Father will not let you." And we are told that not a Christian perished, though great multitudes of other Jews were slaughtered. They fled, and were saved through trusting in God.

Luther stood calm and bold, strong and resolute before his enemies because he believed in God. The arms of faith triumphed over the arms of an empire. Spain marshaled her hosts, built the greatest fleet of ships that ever sailed the waters of the oceans up to that time, and sent the celebrated Spanish Armada to conquer England and bring her down to the foot of the pope again. But that mighty fleet melted away, as it were, like frost before the rising sun, and only a small remnant of it reached home again. God works among the nations. He works in the individual life. All the resources of his kingdom are behind his promises.

Moses feared not the king's wrath, for his heart said, "My Father will not let you." How many times that simple trust in the heart of a helpless saint of God has been mightier than the armies of the kings; has been more powerful than the wills of monarchs! How this works is well illustrated in the case of David and Saul. Saul was a powerful monarch. He had a large army. His army was loyal to him and ready to fight for him. The king was surrounded by guards. He was protected on every hand. No danger was allowed to come nigh him, and yet he was afraid. Afraid of whom? Not afraid of the Philistines; he was ready to go out to fight them. He was not afraid of the Syrians on the north. He was not afraid of being murdered. He was not afraid of a revolt of his army. But Saul was afraid. He was afraid of a man who had no disposition to do him harm. He was afraid of David (I Sam. 18:12). Why did he fear him? For the same reason that a thousand men of high degree have feared those who would not harm them. "And Saul was afraid of David, because the Lord was with him." But David trusted in the Lord; that was the source of his faith. It was his faith that protected him against the wrath of the king. It was his faith that struck with terror the hearts of his enemies. It was his faith that triumphed.

You and I have access to the same God. The power of a living faith in God in us will be the same as in those illustrious examples of past ages. You may find the courage and boldness to say, "My Father won't let you," and believe it in your heart so surely that you can face whatever threatens with a confidence that will not shrink and with a deep, settled satisfaction that the mighty hand of God will not fail to protect and keep you whatever may come.

SUNBURNED CHRISTIANS

DID you ever hear of sunburned Christians? Perhaps you never heard of them spoken of in this way. But I am sure you have seen a number of them. I do not mean that their skins were burned by the sun that shines above us. It is something far more serious than that. I have seen sunburned Christians. I have seen them in all stages of sunburn. Some did not show it very much, and some showed it very strikingly. How much they showed it depended upon the stage their sunburn had reached. Natural sunburn in the tropics often results in death, by bringing on a fatal fever. Spiritual sunburn is very dangerous also. It will produce death too, if proper steps are not taken to cure it before it gets to a fatal stage. So we need to beware of spiritual sunburn. Perhaps some of my readers already have it, and do not know it. Perhaps some of them know something is wrong with them and do not know what it is. I will try to tell you about it.

In Matthew 13:5-6 and Luke 8:6 we read about

these sunburned Christians. It was in the Parable
of the Sower who went forth to sow that Jesus
told us of them. Luke says of the seed, "Some fell
upon a rock; and as soon as it was sprung up, it
withered away, because it lacked moisture." In
other words, this class of people seemed to flourish very well for a while, but presently something
seems to have happened to them. Their greenness
fades. They begin to dry up, and after a while
their spiritual appearance is as sunburned as the
meadows during a drought. You have no doubt
seen places in time of drought where the vegeta-
tion was all dried up and withered away. Everything was sere and brown. There was little to tell
of the abundant life that had been there before.
So it is with some people in their Christian experience.

Jesus interprets his parable thus: "They on the
rock are they, which, when they hear, receive the
word with joy: and these have no root, which for
a while believe, and in time of temptation fall
away." What a contrast this is to the kind of
Christian God expects us to be and the kind that
he provides grace for us to be! Did you know that
God had so provided for us an abundance of grace
that there never has been need that there should

be a single backslider in all the ages since the
gospel was first preached? There has been no
necessity, I say, of there being a single backslider
through all these ages. The gospel teaches the
way of salvation plainly enough. The grace of
God is free enough and abundant enough so that
every soul may serve God acceptably, live victoriously, go on his way triumphant and rejoicing from the time he is saved until he lands safely
in heaven.

The trouble with the seed in the parable was
not that it lacked vitality; for it sprang up. It was
not that some animal came along and ate off its
sprout. It was not that someone dug it up by the
roots. It was not that there was lack of fertility.
The only trouble was that it was on a rock. It
had not much depth of earth. Moisture could not
be brought up by capillary action from the depths
beneath, and so when the moisture in the soil
was dried out by the heat of the sun, the plant
withered, lost its beauty, and became utterly sunburned. But this is not the way that God intends
us to do. He pictures something very different
for us in his Word. Listen to what he says of the
righteous: "He shall be like a tree planted by the
rivers of water, that bringeth forth his fruit in

his season; his leaf also shall not wither; and whatsoever he doeth shall prosper" (Ps. 1:3). Again we read, "And the Lord shall guide thee continually, and satisfy thy soul in drought, and make fat thy bones: and thou shalt be like a watered garden, and like a spring of water, whose waters fail not" (Isa. 58:11). "They shall come and sing in the height of Zion, and shall flow together to the goodness of the Lord, ... and their soul shall be as a watered garden; and they shall not sorrow any more at all" (Jer. 31:12). Note that last statement, "They shall not sorrow any more." That does not mean that they shall not have the usual sorrows of earth, but that they shall not sorrow about their own heart's experience. They shall not say, "Oh, my lack of grace!" "Oh, my weakness!" "Oh, my leanness!" No, they shall not sorrow any more at all, for they shall be "fat and flourishing, to show that the Lord is upright."

Some Christians never get sunburned. Temptation and persecution do not hinder their growth and development. Let the sun shine ever so hot, they only thrive in it. But others get sunburned, wither up, and die. It is the same sun that shines on both. We are told that all things work together for good to them that love the Lord. These difficulties that are encountered by the Christian are only manifestations of God's love towards him. They are intended to promote his growth, to make him stronger in grace, to make him richer in good fruit; and if they are rightly met, they have just this effect. But some cannot meet such things this way. They may try their very best. They will get sunburned in spite of themselves. Why is it? It is because they are upon a rock. They have not much depth of earth.

A rock is a good thing as a foundation for a building, and so we are told to build our house upon a rock; but on a rock is a poor place to raise grain. So if we will bring forth fruit for God we must not be on rocky ground. We must gather out the stones; we must get the soil of our hearts in condition to produce well for God. The experience of some people is no better than it is because they are superficial in their preparation for service to God. They do not go deep enough, and so, although they seem to prosper for a little while, they soon begin to lose their zeal, their earnestness, their spirituality, and in a little while they are gone. Reader, if you feel yourself getting sunburned, begin to explore the soil under you. Begin to examine where your roots are going. You will no doubt find stones in the way.

One stone very common to such people is the love of their own way. They yielded to God to quite an extent under the power of conviction, but not enough really to get crucified to self to the extent that they were truly dead to self, or if they died in the beginning, another stone has formed under them and now they like their own way, and they have their own way more or less. They know what God's way is, but they consciously come a little short of it. They do not measure up to the fullness of what they know they ought. They are not so dead to the world as they should be.

There is another stone that makes some people wither. It is a lack of full submission. They have submitted to God to a considerable extent, but there is a little something held in reserve. Perhaps they are largely unconscious of it, but it is there nevertheless. They have not thrown themselves wholly on the will of God. They are not completely cut loose from self and the world, and so we see the process of sunburning going on in their cases. Others have not measured up to the promises they made to God. When they were seeking

him, they made promises that they would obey
him, that they would make their wrongs right—
that they would do thus and so; but now they
have drawn back. They have put off obedience
from time to time. They have missed opportunities to fulfill their promise. No wonder they are
withering away. No wonder they have a sunburned experience. Some made a full consecration to God, but as time has passed they have
withdrawn it to some extent. Their consecration
is not now so complete as it was, and stone is
forming under them. They will soon dry up and
die.

There are so many who were once flourishing
who are now dried up. They got started all right.
They grew well for a season. But alas, new stones
formed beneath their roots. The moisture was
dried up, and they have withered away. Let us
beware of the stones. Let us see to it that we get
them all out when we start to serve God and that
we keep them out through life. Then we shall
flourish, and the sunshine, the very thing intended to promote growth, will promote it instead of
hindering it and destroying the plant. God will
send the rain and the sunshine; and though the
sun may beat fiercely upon us sometimes, and

though we may have many obstacles, and things may seem to be against us, still, if we trust in God, if we keep all the stones out from beneath us, we shall have plenty of moisture and the hot sun will be a blessing to us. And we shall grow and increase in the Lord, and backsliding will be far from us. But as surely as we let stones rest beneath us, as surely as our consecration does not reach to a proper depth and our life does not measure up to all the truth that we know, we are certain to become sunburned Christians.

WHAT IS THE MATTER WITH ME?

MANY people ask the question, "What is the matter with me?" who are not able to answer it. In some way they do not feel right. There are various symptoms in their feelings that make them think that something is wrong in their spiritual life. Before the trouble is adjusted there is necessity for a right diagnosis. An abnormal condition cannot be treated intelligently unless we know what is causing the condition. The first thing to be decided is, Is anything wrong? There are two kinds of ills—real and imaginary ones. The treatment for the two kinds must be very different. A real illness or disease is supposed to be some abnormal physical condition. Imaginary ills are located in the mind, though when the person becomes convinced he has some sort of ill a physical effect is likely to be produced.

People have imaginary spiritual ills, and not infrequently these imaginary ills give them a great deal of real trouble. The cure for these is to think right, to quit imagining something is wrong when nothing is wrong. An imaginary spiritual trouble may throw the whole spiritual life out of balance and cause untold distress. I have seen many persons who were suffering from imaginary spiritual ills. All they had to do to get the victory and feel all right was to come to realize that the trouble was imaginary, which is no easy thing. But when once this imaginary ill is seen in its right colors and the proper attitude is taken toward it, then normal conditions are quickly restored.

Then there are some who magnify little difficulties into great mountains of trouble. Sometimes persons who have had a little spiritual trouble of some sort magnify it until they come to feel that they are in an almost hopeless situation. They remind me of an experience I had many years ago. I was walking across the country through fields and woods one summer day. Presently one of my toes began to hurt. The farther I went the more it hurt. It felt about as I had heard people say corns feel, so I began to think that I must be getting a corn on my toe. As I walked along and it continued to hurt, in my imagination I could see a corn upon my toe. Finally it hurt so bad that I decided to find out, if possible, what was the trouble. Removing my footwear, I made an examination, but found no corn; instead I found a little thistle spine, almost too small to be seen, sticking in the flesh. This I quickly removed and went on my way without any further trouble. If you mistake some little trifling thing that gives you discomfort in your spiritual life and come to think it a grave evil, you will suffer just as much in your mind as though the trouble were that great evil.

So we need to find out for certain whether our troubles are real or imaginary. Let us note some of the symptoms of trouble that people feel. Sometimes people say, "I don't feel right." When asked what is the matter they say, "Oh, I do not know. I just do not feel right." Sometimes people feel ill at ease spiritually, unsatisfied, sometimes a flood of doubts comes into the mind, sometimes there are fears. The person fears and knows not what he is fearing. He fears he is not right. He fears this, that, or the other thing, but does not know whether things are thus or not. Sometimes there is a sense of spiritual weakness, a feeling of inability to accomplish anything in spiritual matters. Sometimes one gets to where he cannot pray, or do so only with difficulty, and his prayers seem mechanical and formal. Sometimes there is a sense of oppression that settles down on one; he is in heaviness and perplexity. Sometimes a feeling of condemnation comes upon people; perhaps they do not feel right, yet know nothing that they have done that is wrong. They search and search and find nothing at all, and still they have a feeling of condemnation. Others search and find little trifling things, things for which they would not think of condemning anyone else, yet they themselves feel condemned. They are troubled and perplexed.

Again there are times when a sense of loneliness settles down upon one. I knew a lady who used to sing the song, "I Am Never Lonely Any More Since the Comforter Has Come." Then she herself would have lonely spells and would have a feeling of condemnation because she felt she should not feel lonely when the Holy Spirit was with her. There are also times when people have a feeling of apprehension as though something evil were going to happen. They feel troubled and bothered, and do not know what to do. There are others who feel tried, and hardly know at what they are tried; but they have a deep sense of being tried. There are many other things, too, which give people trouble. They are all indications of something. But we have many feelings the origin of which we cannot determine. Sometimes the feelings of oppression and condemnation, heaviness, apprehension, and such like, of which we have been speaking, come directly from Satan, or from the influence of demons about us, or from the influence of people who are evil. And sometimes it is the influence upon us of others who have similar feelings.

There are those who used to have no trouble, but now they do have trouble with their feelings, and they ask the question, "What is the matter with me? I did not used to be bothered this way." Let us look at a few things that cause people trouble in their spiritual life. First is a lack of steadfast faith. Sometimes people let doubts creep in when there are no real grounds for doubting one's experience. The simple, steadfast faith that they had at first they do not hold. They let questionings come in. Just as soon as we question ourselves whether we are right or not, we relax our steadfast faith and let doubt come in. And then, of course, we cannot feel the same as we did before. Many young converts do this. They feel joyous at first. Their faith is steadfast and unshaken. They know they are safe. But presently they come to question themselves, "Why do I feel this way?" Then when doubt enters certainty goes, trouble begins, and unless they get to believing steadfastly again they are likely to have an unsettled experience. If you have let doubt come in as to your experience, you need not expect to feel as you did before until you are rid of the doubt. When you believe as simply and as steadfastly as you did before, you will feel all right again.

Sometimes people make failures in what they attempt. They come short of their expectations, and then condemnation, doubts, fears, and such like come upon them. In such cases it is only the discouragement of their failure and their letting down in faith that troubles them. Let them renew their confidence and go forward, and they will be all right.

Another thing that is the source of much spiritual trouble is the withdrawing of one's consecration. When we make a full consecration to God, it brings us into a sacred relationship with him. When we draw back or drift back from this consecration, it paves the way for all sorts of troubles. If we are troubled, we need first to examine our consecration and see that it is full and up to date. If it is not, bring it there. Neglect of duty also is a thing that often gets people into trouble. Through timidity or fear or sheer neglect they let opportunities and duties pass. This often brings condemnation. It weakens and troubles.

Another cause of trouble is partaking of things the conscience does not approve fully. When the conscience is wounded, it reacts on confidence. Some people allow and do things now that they formerly would not do. Perhaps the change has been all right. Perhaps it has not. "Happy is he that condemneth not himself in that thing which he alloweth." Many people's troubles and spiritual lacks are to be located along this line. The cause is that they do not keep their conscience in a proper attitude and do not live up to its requirements.

Another cause of trouble is not heeding spiritual warnings or urgings. Some people ask, "Why does not God show me things as he used to do?" Perhaps it is because they did not heed what he showed them before.

Whatever is the matter with you in your feelings or in your experience, find out the cause if possible; or if you cannot find out the cause, begin to go over your consecration. Draw near to God, stir up your faith to activity, reject your doubts, believe God, measure up to all the truth you know, and then cast yourself full length on God's mercy and trust him for all you need. The Great Physician can cure all your spiritual ills if you will submit to him.

IF YE FORGIVE

ONE of the most striking things that Jesus taught was that we should forgive our enemies, and not only forgive them but also adopt an attitude toward them that indicates a complete change of feeling toward them. He came to break down the middle wall of partition, not merely between the Jews and Gentiles in the national sense or in the religious sense, but also in the personal sense he breaks down all walls that have been built up to separate the hearts of people. The mercy that God shows in forgiving us puts us under the most solemn obligation to forgive others. Many people find this the hardest of all things to do. But God tells us plainly that if we will not forgive others we cannot be forgiven. If we will not forgive men, he will not forgive us. Forgiveness, therefore, is a part of true repentance, and repentance is not complete until the heart adopts the forgiving attitude toward every enemy; and not only forgives because it feels it must, but also because it is disposed to forgive when it once has been forgiven and the love of God has come into the heart.

God is disposed to forgive his enemies. He is so much disposed to do it that he sought a means whereby he could safely do so. He was so disposed to forgive a trespass against himself that he gave his Son so that he might forgive transgressors. He was disposed to forgive so that he would make any sacrifice in order to be able to forgive, and not have his forgiveness turn out badly. He sent his Son into the world to make forgiveness possible with safety by changing the heart of the individual forgiven. But we cannot take any such precaution. That is quite beyond our power. More than that, there is no need of such action on our part for God has already, through his Son, done all that is necessary. So he teaches us to forgive, and to leave all consequences in his hand.

Many persons say, "I just cannot forgive." This is true even to professors of religion. And many of them, though they do say so, do not really forgive, for the thing still rankles in their hearts. How different is their attitude from God's! He *wants* to forgive. They will hardly forgive even under strong pressure, then many times their forgiveness is only from the lips. We find many professors of religion who are prejudiced against people. This prejudice is manifested in a disposition to believe evil of them, or to put an unfavorable construction upon what they do or say. A lack of fairness is shown, and not unfrequently a disposition to be rather elated when anything unpleasant happens to them. Back of such a prejudice lies a wrong attitude of heart, an unchristian attitude.

It matters not what an individual has done or said about us, nor what his attitude is toward us, if we hold the Christian attitude toward him we shall feel a disposition to be perfectly fair with him. Perhaps we have a cause of complaint against him. Perhaps his conduct has not been and is not what it should be toward us. But if we have a forgiving spirit clear down to the depths of our hearts we will hold that same attitude of kindness and pity that Jesus held toward those who did wrong toward him, and that he holds toward sinners now. While we hate his evil-doing, we nevertheless feel no animosity toward him. But if we are prejudiced against him, if we will not give him a fair show, then we have reason to question the genuineness of our disposition to forgive.

Sometimes this lack of forgiving disposition is manifested in the home. There is ill feeling, unpleasantness, a disposition toward criticism and faultfinding. The members of the same family, who ought to love and feel a real tenderness toward each other, are often alienated. Sometimes that alienation grows until it rankles in the heart. But notwithstanding this, the individuals may consider themselves very good Christians. Perhaps they throw all the blame upon the other one, but the old saying is, "It takes two to make a quarrel." In the same way it takes two to make ill feeling between two persons. "Charity suffereth long, and is kind." That divine charity or love that is shed abroad in our hearts issues invariably in a disposition to be forgiving. What is needed in many families is forgiveness. Feelings will be hurt, supposed rights will be trampled upon, consciously or unconsciously, offense will be given sometimes. The question is, will we forgive these things, or will we let them start a canker in our hearts? We need to take antiseptic precautions for our heart as well as for our body, to protect ourselves against the germs of evil as we try to protect ourselves against the germs of disease. But the question comes up square to face us: do we forgive in our home circle?

If there is a reconciliation between parties who have been at enmity, that reconciliation is based on forgiveness; and when the forgiveness is genuine there is a complete restoration of friendship and unity between the parties. Where such restoration does not come as the result of the attempt to right matters, there is only one reason why it does not. That reason is, there has been no forgiveness. Where people really forgive each other there is nothing that remains to be taken out of the way. There is nothing rankling in the heart; there is nothing to push the other off; there is none of that "keep your distance" air; there is no feeling of coldness. An unforgiving disposition is at the bottom of almost all church troubles, and it is of no use to attempt to talk such things out of the way. People cannot be talked together; they cannot be argued together; there is only one thing that will bring them together, and that is for all to show a genuinely forgiving spirit. This leaves nothing to be a source of disturbance.

Why is it that people will not forgive? Is it because others have treated them wrongfully? Is it because their attitude toward them is not proper? No, it is nothing like this, though all this may have occurred. It is not what the other fellow has done; it is what is in our hearts that prevents forgiveness. If we will not forgive, it is because we are proud, stubborn, and self-willed. It is never hard to forgive when our own hearts adopt a proper attitude. Like God, then we *desire* to forgive. But do not overlook this one thing: forgiveness issues in peace, at least in a peaceful heart for the one who forgives, and in a Christlike attitude toward the wrongdoer. Where this Christlike attitude does not exist there is no forgiveness. In the church where things are settled and then come up again to trouble, or where coldness, indifference, and lack of love are manifested, forgiveness is the one thing needed in the hearts of those who hold such an attitude.

A good lesson was impressed upon my mind when I looked in my concordance to see what was said in the Bible on this subject. I found the word "forgave," then after it the word "forget," and on a little way the word "forgive." As "forget" stood right in the midst of "forgiveness" in my concordance, so it stands in the human heart. Forget is right in the heart of forgive; and if it is not that way in our hearts and minds, it is because the right attitude is not in our hearts.

If it is so hard for some to forgive once, how do they expect to carry out Christ's injunction to forgive seventy times seven? Let us examine our hearts. Let us inquire whether we have a forgiving spirit, remembering the while that a forgiving spirit does not abide in the same heart with hatred, bitterness, hardness and prejudice against people. When we forgive people it softens our hearts toward them. When we are reconciled to God, what blessedness it brings! When we are reconciled to our enemies, we partake of that same blessedness in our own hearts that we have when we are reconciled to Christ. But if we forgive not we shall not be forgiven, and our hearts will be fertile soil to receive all the seeds of evil that Satan would sow therein.

TURNING ON THE LIGHT

THE dense black clouds rolled up from the west, obscuring the sky, shutting out the light and making it so dark I could no longer see to work. My wife walked over to the center of the room and turned the switch on the lamp and instantly the room was flooded with light. We know in our home there is a way to produce light any time we wish to do so. We know just what to do to produce that light. When we do that thing we expect the light, but one noticeable thing is that the light does not shine until it is turned on. It requires something on our part in order to bring about its shining. If we did not do that thing we could not have the light no matter how much current there was in the wire nor how good a lamp might be in the socket.

Now, spiritual life and experience are very much like temporal life and experience. The same principles hold good in both. But will a Christian ever get in darkness? Will not his pathway always be illuminated by the light of heaven?

For some time past a man has been trying to convince me that a Christian should never go into darkness, that we should always be in the light. Well, that would be fine were it true, but when we read the Bible we find that people did not always have such an experience. We know that Job was a righteous man, but he passed through a time of terrible darkness. He suffered many things he could not understand; he had many experiences he thought he ought not to have had. The Psalmist cries out of darkness, and sometimes almost out of despair. The New Testament speaks of being in heaviness through manifold temptations, and of being tried by strange things.

But why should a Christian have seasons of darkness? For the same reason that my light was shut off by the clouds so that I could not work; that is, circumstances combine in such a way as to produce the darkness. It was no fault of mine that I could not see. I had not sinned against the Lord that he sent the clouds. Sometimes I do pull down the shade and shut out the light, so Christians sometimes do things that shut out the light, but many times the light is shut out by circumstances that arise through no fault of the one experiencing the darkness. But does not

the Bible say that "he that followeth me shall
not walk in darkness, but shall have the light
of life"? To be sure it says that, and it speaks
truly. We are not in darkness in the sense of being
without God's light upon our souls. We know his
truth, and his Spirit illuminates our souls. The
sun shines upon this planet all the time; it is
never obscured only in an eclipse and then only
a small portion of the surface of the world is affected. But it happens that we are not always on
the side of the earth on which it is shining. We
are in darkness almost half of the time, and yet
the sun is shining continually. The trouble is the
earth gets between us and the sun by turning
around with its other side to the sun. Circumstances have a way of turning us around sometimes so that the light of God, be it ever so bright,
cannot for the time fall upon us. We are left in
the shadow of those circumstances that come in
our lives and we cannot help it.

But how can one be in God's light and in
darkness at the same time? Just the same way
that a man can be in the darkness and in the light
when he takes a lantern and goes forth on a
dark night. When we get on the shadowy side of a
circumstance, instead of despairing we should

light our lantern or turn on our electric light. Before we notice how to do this let us look a little further at the way people who are good Christians sometimes get into darkness. In the first place, darkness comes from unexpected circumstances or from circumstances over which we have no control. Sorrow comes to us unbidden. Death invades the family circle; losses come in business; misunderstandings arise; we may be blamed for things for which we are not guilty; trials may come that we do not understand; our joy may take wings, and heaviness may settle down upon us. We may come to a place where prayer is difficult or impossible and when we try to pray our words mock us. Do I hear someone exclaim, "A Christian never gets into such a situation!" Well, maybe you never have, but I have. I have had the experience more than once. I have known many others to have such experiences.

Under such circumstances many people become discouraged. That is not the proper thing to do. When darkness comes, turn on the light. Job had seen dark places before, but none of them had ever been so dark as the one in which he found himself in his special time of trial. He said, "Oh that I were as in months past, as in the days when God preserved me; when his candle shined upon my head, and when by his light I walked through darkness" (Job 29:2-3). Now he was in darkness in which God's light did not seem to shine, still he was a righteous man. God himself said so. Here is a promise to those who are walking in darkness, "Unto the upright there ariseth light in the darkness" (Ps. 112:4). This shows that even the upright get into places where they need light, and here is a promise in which to trust when we are in such a place. Sometimes we are like Job said of himself, "When I looked for good, then evil came unto me: and when I waited for light, there came darkness" (Job 30:26).

We do not always get out of darkness at once. Sometimes we pray and no answer seems to come. God wants us to continue to endure. He desires us to hold fast our faith in him and in ourselves. No matter even if our darkness has been caused by some fault of our own, hold fast to our confidence in God; hold fast to what good things there are in you and turn on the light. You may have to grope in the darkness for a while before you find where to turn on the light and how to do it. Nevertheless, if you persevere you will find the way, and the light will come. You have already within you the light of life that God gives to all that are saved. God will keep that shining no matter how dark external circumstances may be.

In the darkest hour we may turn to God's lamp, for the Psalmist has said, "Thy word is a lamp unto my feet, and a light unto my path." So, in your trouble turn to the Word of God. Read its promises. Behold in it the mercies of God: his faithfulness, his loyalty to his own. Take his Word for your light and for the basis of your hope. No matter how dark things may look, God's Word is true to you just as it was to Job, to Abraham, to David, and to millions of others. We turn on light from heaven by believing in God, trusting in his loving-kindness with confidence. The Psalmist said, "They looked unto him, and were radiant" (Ps. 34:5, A. R. V.). They were radiant; that is, the light shone round about them and it shone from within themselves. When the light of joy comes into the soul how quickly the things about us, no matter what their nature, are illuminated!